THE INVISIBLE INFLUENCE

Unveiling the Power of Faceless YouTube Success

BY
NIALL BROWNE

Copyright 2024 Niall Browne. All rights reserved.

No part of this book may be reproduced in any form or by any electronic or mechanical means including information storage and retrieval systems, without permission in writing from the author. The only exception is by a reviewer, who may quote short excerpts in a review.

Although the author and publisher have made every effort to ensure that the information in this book was correct at press time, the author and publisher do not assume and hereby disclaim any liability to any party for any loss, damage, or disruption caused by errors or omissions, whether such errors or omissions result from negligence, accident, or any other cause.

This publication is designed to provide accurate and authoritative information with regard to the subject matter covered. It is sold with the understanding that the publisher is not engaged in rendering professional services. If legal advice or other expert assistance is required, the services of a competent professional should be sought.

The fact that an organization or website is referred to in this work as a citation and/or a potential source of further information does not mean that the author or the publisher endorses the information the organization or website may provide or recommendations it may make.

Please remember that Internet websites listed in this work may have changed or disappeared between when this work was written and when it is read.

TABLE OF CONTENTS

Introduction 4

Chapter 1: Finding Your Niche 14

Chapter 2: Crafting Your Strategy 27

Chapter 3: Setting Up Your Channel 39

Chapter 4: Content Creation and Production 51

Chapter 5: Optimizing Videos for SEO 66

Chapter 6: Uploading and Publishing Videos 79

Chapter 7: Growing and Engaging Your Audience 92

Chapter 8: Monetization Strategies 105

Chapter 9: Creating Passive Income Streams 117

Chapter 10: Staying Ahead of the Curve 129

Chapter 11: Case Studies and Success Stories 142

Conclusion 152

Introduction

Welcome to the exciting world of faceless YouTube channels, where the potential to carve out your digital empire and generate passive income lies right at your fingertips. Imagine creating content that resonates, entertains, and educates, all while keeping your identity a mystery. This dynamic space has opened doors for countless creators to share their passions and expertise without the need for personal recognition. Here, the focus shifts from the creator to the content, allowing for a unique blend of creativity and anonymity. Whether you're here to explore a hobby, share knowledge, or kickstart a side hustle, this book is your all-in-one guide. We're going to navigate the bustling streets of YouTube together, uncovering the secrets to building a successful faceless channel. From discovering your niche to perfecting your content strategy, and monetizing your efforts, we've got you covered. So, let's dive in and turn those ideas into reality, transforming your creative vision into a thriving online presence.

The Rise of Faceless YouTube Channels

In recent years, the landscape of YouTube has undergone a fascinating transformation, welcoming the rise of faceless YouTube channels. These channels, often run by individuals who prefer to remain anonymous, have captivated a vast audience by focusing on high-quality content over personal vlogging and face-centric videos. This shift has not only expanded the creative horizon but also opened up a realm of opportunities for creators looking to forge a presence on YouTube without stepping into the limelight.

The concept of faceless YouTube channels is intriguing, primarily because it challenges the traditional notion that personal branding is the only path to success on the platform. Creators have now found a way to make their mark by producing content that ranges from storytelling and educational videos to animations and commentary, all without revealing their identity. It's a testament to the power of content quality and the universality of themes that resonate with a wide audience.

One of the key drivers behind the rise of these channels is the desire for privacy and the ability to create without the pressure of public scrutiny. In an era where online privacy concerns are at their peak, the option to remain faceless is not only appealing but empowering for many. It enables creators to share their work with the world while preserving their personal space and anonymity.

Beyond privacy, the appeal of faceless channels also lies in their versatility and the potential for scalability. Without being tied to a specific person, these channels can explore a broader range of topics, adapt to changing trends more swiftly, and even involve multiple creators, making content production more efficient and diverse. This flexibility is a significant asset in the ever-evolving landscape of YouTube, where audience preferences and algorithmic priorities can shift rapidly.

Moreover, the success of faceless channels has highlighted the audience's appetite for varied content. Viewers are drawn to the quality of information, storytelling prowess, and the uniqueness of the content rather than the charisma and personality of the creator. This shift signifies a more inclusive environment where the merit of content reigns supreme, providing an equal footing for all creators, regardless of their on-screen presence.

Financially, faceless channels offer a lucrative pathway for creators. With the potential to attract substantial viewership and engagement, these channels can tap into the vast revenue opportunities available on

YouTube, from ad revenue and sponsorships to merchandise sales and affiliate marketing, all while maintaining the creators' anonymity.

For those contemplating starting a faceless YouTube channel, the process might seem daunting initially. Yet, it opens up a world of creativity and innovation. The focus shifts to crafting compelling narratives, finding unique angles for popular topics, and utilizing visual and auditory elements to engage the audience. This creative freedom is a significant draw for many aspiring creators.

However, building a successful faceless channel is not without its challenges. It demands a keen understanding of SEO, mastery of storytelling and editing, and an ability to stay aligned with what the audience craves, all without the innate draw of a personal brand. But for those willing to navigate these waters, the rewards can be both fulfilling and financially rewarding.

In the pages that follow, we will delve into the strategies and insights that can help you master the art of creating a successful faceless YouTube channel. From defining your niche and developing a content strategy to optimizing your videos for SEO and engaging your audience, the goal is to provide a roadmap that empowers you to build and grow your channel with confidence.

The landscape of YouTube is vast, and the rise of faceless channels is a compelling evolution that has democratized content creation. It underscores the idea that anyone, irrespective of their desire to be in the spotlight, can create content that resonates, entertains, and informs. The key lies in understanding your strengths, the needs of your audience, and the endless possibilities that this platform offers.

As we embark on this journey together, remember that the success of your faceless YouTube channel hinges on your passion, persistence, and willingness to learn and adapt. It's about finding what you love, sharing it with the world in your unique way, and building a community around your content. The path might be paved with challenges, but the potential rewards, both personal and financial, are immense.

Let this rise of faceless YouTube channels serve as inspiration for what you can achieve. In a world where authenticity and quality content are king, there's never been a better time to venture into the unknown and create something truly remarkable. Your channel could be the next big thing on YouTube, and the journey starts now.

So let's dive in, explore the intricacies of creating compelling content without showing your face, and unlock the secrets to building a successful, sustainable faceless YouTube channel. The journey ahead is exciting, and the opportunities are limitless. Are you ready to make your mark on YouTube and create a passive income stream that thrives? The time is now, and the possibilities are yours for the taking.

Why Faceless Channels are Trending

You might be wondering what's the big deal with faceless YouTube channels? Why are they gaining so much traction? The trend is real, and it's reshaping the landscape of content creation on one of the world's biggest platforms. In this section, we'll dive deep into the why's and how's, uncovering the secret sauce that makes these channels so appealing.

First up, privacy. In an era where digital footprints are closely scrutinized, the allure of anonymity is stronger than ever. Content creators are finding solace in the fact that they can produce engaging content without putting their personal lives under the microscope. This is a game-changer for many, especially those who value their privacy but still want to share their passion and expertise with the world.

Then there's the scalability factor. Faceless channels typically rely on voiceovers, animations, stock footage, and other forms of content that don't require a physical presence. This means creators can churn out high-quality videos at a pace that would be hard to match if they had to be in front of the camera. Plus, they can manage multiple channels across various niches, significantly amplifying their earning potential.

Cost-efficiency plays a huge role too. Starting a traditional YouTube channel can be expensive. There's the cost of decent filming equipment, lighting, maybe even a studio setup. Faceless channels, on the other hand, often require less upfront investment. Software for animations, voice modulation, and editing are generally more affordable and accessible, lowering the barrier to entry for new creators.

Let's talk about the creative freedom that comes with running a faceless channel. Without the need to appear on camera, creators can experiment with different styles, formats, and subjects. This freedom encourages innovation and allows for a broader range of content, which can be both refreshing and engaging for an audience seeking something new and different.

Audience appeal is another crucial element. Viewers are increasingly gravitating towards content that is informative, entertaining, and easily digestible. Faceless channels often hit all these marks, offering viewers an escape into worlds crafted through animations, compelling narrations, and curated visuals that traditional vlogging can't always provide.

Global reach is yet another advantage. Since faceless channels can produce content that's not bound by a specific language or culture, they have the potential to appeal to a global audience. With the right translation and subtitle strategies, these channels can cross geographical and linguistic barriers, unlocking vast audiences and diverse revenue streams.

Consistency in branding and presentation is easier to maintain with faceless channels. Without the need to be physically present, creators can ensure a consistent look and feel across all videos, which helps in building a strong, recognizable brand. This consistency aids in viewer retention and loyalty, key ingredients for long-term success on the platform.

Then there's adaptability. The digital landscape is always changing, and faceless channels are in a prime position to pivot quickly. Whether it's a new trend, algorithm update, or platform feature, these channels can adapt their content more swiftly without the constraints of traditional video production.

Another draw is the potential for longevity. Faceless channels can continue to produce content without worrying about the personal circumstances of the creator that might affect on-camera channels. This can lead to a more sustainable and long-lasting presence on YouTube, which is essential for building a passive income stream.

The anonymity aspect also protects creators from burnout and public scrutiny. Managing a personal brand can be exhausting, with the pressure to constantly share one's life and face criticism or judgment. Faceless channels sidestep this issue, enabling creators to focus purely on their content and creative output.

Moreover, faceless channels appeal to a wide range of creators, from introverts who may feel uncomfortable appearing on camera to professionals seeking to share their expertise without personal branding. This inclusivity is a significant factor in the growing trend of faceless channels.

Then there's the matter of content legacy. Videos on faceless channels are often evergreen, covering topics that remain relevant over time. This ensures a steady flow of views and income long after the videos are published, contributing to the channel's sustainability and the creator's financial security.

Lastly, faceless channels offer a unique way to tell stories and educate. Without the focus on a personal brand, the content itself takes center stage. This shift allows creators to delve deeper into their subjects, exploring angles and narratives that might be overlooked in personality-driven channels.

In sum, the trend towards faceless YouTube channels is driven by a complex interplay of privacy, cost, creativity, audience demand, and the evolving nature of digital content consumption. As we move forward, it's clear that these channels represent not just a fleeting trend, but a substantial shift in how content is created and consumed on one of the world's largest platforms.

Understanding the 'why' behind faceless channels is just the beginning. Next, we'll explore how you can harness this trend to build your own successful channel, creating content that resonates and generates income while keeping your privacy intact. It's a thrilling journey ahead, and the potential is as vast as your imagination.

How This Book Will Help You Succeed

Unleashing the full potential of a faceless YouTube channel might sound like a daunting task, but that's exactly where this book steps in. It's tailored to cut through the noise and offer crystal clear guidance on making your mark in the digital world without ever having to show your face. Let's dive into how this guide is your ticket to success in this arena.

Firstly, understanding the landscape is crucial. You might be wondering how you can stand out in a sea of content. This book lays down the groundwork by helping you navigate through the intricacies of YouTube's algorithm, ensuring your content reaches the right eyes. But it's not just about getting your videos out there; it's about captivating your audience. Through the pages, you'll discover the secrets to crafting content that resonates, keeps viewers coming back, and turns casual views into a dedicated community.

Moreover, we delve deep into the strategic side of things. Sure, creating content is fun, but doing it with a strategic mindset? That's what sets the pros apart. We'll dissect the anatomy of successful faceless channels, leaving you with actionable insights to design a content strategy that aligns with your goals – whether that's building a loyal fanbase, generating passive income, or both.

Let's talk technical for a moment. Equipment and software might seem like hurdles, but in reality, they're your allies. This book simplifies the vast ocean of editing tools, recording equipment, and software, guiding you to make choices that are effective yet budget-friendly. It's about being smart, not splashing cash unnecessarily.

Then, there's the art of optimization. From keywords that boost your visibility to thumbnails that grab attention, understanding YouTube SEO is non-negotiable. You'll learn to master these elements, enhancing your video's chances to appear in search results and suggested video feeds. It's like giving your content its very own spotlight.

Engagement is the name of the game. If you're looking to build a faceless channel, understanding how to engage and grow your audience without revealing your identity adds an extra layer of challenge – but it's nothing you can't handle with the strategies outlined in this book. From interactive polls to captivating storytelling, we've got you covered.

Making money through your channel might seem like a distant dream, but it's closer than you think. We explore various monetization strategies beyond the obvious. Think affiliate marketing, digital products, and even exclusive content subscriptions. This book provides you with the blueprint to diversify your income streams, ensuring you're not putting all your eggs in one basket.

Passive income is the ultimate goal, right? Setting up systems that earn you money while you sleep might sound too good to be true, but it's entirely achievable with faceless YouTube channels. We'll walk you through automating revenue models, content syndication, and more, painting a clear picture of how to sustain and scale your earnings over time.

But what about the long run? Staying ahead of the curve is critical. YouTube is an ever-evolving platform, and your ability to adapt and innovate is key to ongoing success. This book doesn't just prepare you for today; it equips you with the mindset and tactics to evolve and thrive in the future of digital content creation.

Throughout this journey, we've emphasized not just the 'how' but also the 'why.' By understanding the rationale behind each strategy, you're empowered to think critically, adapt, and even innovate beyond what you learn here. It's not just about following a set path; it's about charting your own course to success.

Coated with motivational undertones, every chapter is designed to boost your confidence. Overcoming self-doubt and the fear of starting something new can be challenging, but remember, every big creator started with zero subscribers. This book is your cheerleader, reminding you that with persistence and the right strategies, you're poised for greatness.

Finally, this book stands as a testament to the idea that anyone can succeed on YouTube, faceless or not. Your ideas, creativity, and passion are valid and deserving of a platform. By focusing on your strengths and following the guidance laid out in these pages, you're not just setting up a channel; you're setting up a legacy.

In conclusion, 'How This Book Will Help You Succeed' is not just a promise; it's a proven roadmap. With each chapter meticulously crafted to address every aspect of building and growing a faceless YouTube channel, you're equipped with the knowledge, skills, and motivation needed to turn your vision into reality. It's time to embark on this exciting journey, and we can't wait to see where it takes you.

Remember, success is not an accident. It's the result of deliberate decisions, strategies, and actions. This book is your guide, your mentor, and your plan. Immerse yourself in these pages, apply the lessons, and let's build something incredible together.

Chapter 1

Finding Your Niche

So, you've gotten a good grip on why faceless YouTube channels are a goldmine for creators looking to generate passive income, huh? Now, the journey begins with arguably the most crucial step: finding your niche. Think of your niche not just as a topic area but as your secret sauce, the unique flavor you'll add to the YouTube universe. It's all about marrying your passion and expertise with what the market is eager to consume. This isn't about casting a wide net and hoping for the best; it's laser-targeting an audience that shares your interests or needs the knowledge you possess.

But where do you start? Dive deep into your personal interests and skills, then match them against the current market trends and demands. It's like being a detective in your own life, figuring out what you're brilliantly good at, or what excites you the most, and then validating those ideas against what people are actively searching for. You'll also be sizing up the competition to see where you can carve out your own space. Aren't you a bit curious to see successful examples? We'll also explore case studies of faceless channels that have nailed their niche, offering that spark of inspiration to kickstart your brainstorming process. Finding your niche is the foundation upon which your channel's success will be built, so let's dig in and discover where you can make your mark.

Identifying Your Passion and Expertise

When diving into the world of faceless YouTube channels, the cornerstone of your success lies in pinpointing your passion and expertise. This initial step is crucial, as it not only sets the direction for your content but also ensures you're engaging in work that truly resonates with you. Let's embark on discovering how to unlock these elements within yourself to set a solid foundation for your channel.

Firstly, let's talk about passion. It's that fiery drive inside you, something you can discuss, explore, and create content about for hours on end without losing interest. Have you ever caught yourself losing track of time when immersed in a particular activity or topic? That's a giveaway you've hit upon a passion. However, it's vital to note that passion alone isn't enough. The true magic happens when you marry your passion with expertise.

Expertise, in contrast to passion, is cultivated. It's the accumulation of knowledge and skills in a specific domain where you have significant experience. This doesn't mean you have to be the absolute best in your field, but having a deep understanding and unique insights to share is key.

Combining passion with expertise allows you to create content that's not only engaging but also valuable and unique. This unique blend is what will distinguish your channel in the bustling universe of YouTube. It positions you as a go-to source for viewers seeking content that's both informative and enlightening.

Many people struggle with identifying their passion or expertise, but there are several exercises and questions that can help unlock these insights. Start by reflecting on your current hobbies, interests, and the types of books, articles, or videos you consume. What topics do you find yourself drawn to? What activities make you lose track of time? Digging into these areas can unearth hidden passions.

Next, consider the skills or knowledge areas where others frequently seek your advice. These can be indicators of your expertise. This could range from digital marketing strategies to video game tips, DIY home decor, or even wellness practices. Sometimes, the very expertise we take for granted is what others are eager to learn about.

Mind mapping can also be an invaluable tool in this phase. Creating a visual representation of your interests and areas of knowledge can highlight potential niches that intersect with your passion and expertise. This method can unveil a plethora of ideas that you might not have considered otherwise.

Don't rush this process. Identifying your passion and expertise is a journey that requires introspection and patience. It's about digging deep to understand what truly motivates you and how you can leverage your strengths and interests to create compelling content.

Once you've pinpointed a potential niche that aligns with your passion and expertise, it's crucial to validate it. This involves ensuring there's an audience for your content and that it has the potential to grow. We'll delve deeper into researching market demand and trends in the following sections, but keep in mind that your chosen niche should excite you and appeal to a specific audience.

Remember, your passion is your fuel, and your expertise is your vehicle. Together, they enable you to navigate the YouTube arena with authenticity and authority. While the road ahead may have its challenges, starting with a strong foundation rooted in your passion and expertise will make the journey not just successful, but also incredibly fulfilling.

It's also worth noting that passions and expertise can evolve. As you grow and explore different facets of your chosen niche, new interests may spark, and your knowledge will expand. Embrace this evolution, as it's an opportunity to refresh your content and keep your audience engaged. Always be open to learning and exploring new horizons within your niche.

Lastly, don't let the fear of saturation deter you. Even if there are many creators in your niche, your unique perspective and insights can carve out a distinct space for your channel. It's your individuality, combined with your passion and expertise, that will attract like-minded viewers to your content.

Identifying your passion and expertise is the first, pivotal step on your journey to building a successful faceless YouTube channel. It lays the groundwork for creating content that's not only fulfilling to produce but also resonates deeply with your audience. Keep this foundation strong, and you'll be well on your way to achieving excellence in the faceless YouTube realm.

In conclusion, this exploration into your inner drivers and skills is more than just a preparatory step; it's a strategic move towards establishing a profound connection with your audience. By aligning your content with what you love and know best, you're poised to create a channel that stands out, inspires, and ultimately thrives.

Researching Market Demand and Trends

After figuring out what fires you up, it's time to dive deep into the waters of market demand and trends. This is where you turn that spark of passion into a firecracker of success in the YouTube universe. Remember, even if your idea feels unique, understanding the landscape can vastly improve your chances of creating a channel that not only resonates with viewers but also stands the test of time.

Let's start with the basics: market demand. This means finding out if people are actually searching for content within your niche. It might surprise you, but even the most obscure topics can have a bustling audience online. The key is knowing where to look. Google Trends and the YouTube search bar are your best friends here. Punch in keywords related to your niche and see what comes up. A healthy volume of searches indicates a hungry audience waiting to devour your content.

But it's not all about numbers; it's also about understanding the pulse of your potential viewers. Trends ebb and flow, and what's hot today might be forgotten tomorrow. Subscribing to industry newsletters, following relevant social media groups, and keeping an eye on what's trending on YouTube itself can give you invaluable insight into what content is likely to resonate with audiences, both now and in the future.

While researching, you might notice certain patterns emerging. Maybe there's a rise in educational content in your field, or perhaps entertainment videos related to your niche are getting more traction. These patterns are gold mines for a new creator. They can help you tailor your content not just to what you love to talk about, but to what people love to watch.

Another key point is to gauge the seasonality of your chosen niche. Some topics may soar in popularity during certain times of the year and plummet in others. By identifying these trends, you can plan your content calendar more effectively, ensuring you're always ahead of the curve and ready to capture your audience's attention at just the right time.

Next up, let's talk about competition. Yes, seeing a lot of channels covering your niche might seem daunting, but it's actually a good sign. It means there's a proven audience for your content. The trick is to find a gap in what's being offered. What unique angle or perspective can you bring to the table? This is where your creativity and passion become your biggest assets.

However, analyzing the competition isn't just about figuring out how you can be different. It's also about learning from what others are doing right (and wrong). Watch popular videos in your niche and read the comments. What are viewers loving, and what are they asking for more of? This feedback is a direct line to your audience's desires and a surefire way to ensure your content hits the mark.

Now, let's not forget about leveraging keywords and SEO (Search Engine Optimization). Knowing which keywords are most searched can help you craft not only your videos but also your titles, descriptions, and even the tags you use. This small but crucial step ensures that your videos are discoverable, driving organic traffic to your channel.

Identifying trends early can give you a significant advantage as well. YouTube, like all social media platforms, is always evolving. New types of content can emerge as trends almost overnight. By staying informed and adaptable, you can be at the forefront of these trends, catapulting your channel to popularity by meeting viewer demands before they even fully realize them themselves.

It's also important to consider the broader context of your niche within the global digital landscape. With audiences from around the world, understanding cultural shifts, global events, and even emerging technologies can influence the direction of your content. This broader perspective ensures your channel remains relevant and engaging to a wide audience.

Engagement metrics also offer a wealth of information. Once you start publishing content, keeping an eye on your video performance can give you real-time feedback on what works. High watch times, likes, and shares are indicators that you're on the right track. Conversely, a high number of dislikes or negative comments can provide valuable lessons on what to improve.

Collaborating with other creators in your niche can also provide insights and boost your visibility. Not only can you tap into each other's audiences, but you can also exchange ideas and strategies for tackling the market. Collaborations can be a powerful tool for gaining insights into what your shared audience craves.

Constant learning and evolution are the name of the game when it comes to YouTube success. No channel, no matter how big, ever stops adapting. The landscape is constantly shifting, and so should your approach. Feedback loops from your audience, ongoing trend research, and occasional pivots based on what you learn are essential for long-term growth.

Finding your niche and making it big on YouTube is about blending what you love with what the market wants. It's about finding that sweet spot where your passion meets audience demand. Remember, every successful YouTuber started exactly where you are now. With diligent research, a pulse on trends, and a commitment to delivering value, there's no limit to what you can achieve.

So, keep pushing, keep researching, and most importantly, keep creating. The next viral faceless YouTube channel could very well be yours. Armed with the insights on market demand and trends, you're now poised to carve out your unique space in the vast YouTube ecosystem. Go out there and make waves.

Evaluating Competition and Opportunities

Stepping into the YouTube arena, especially when you're leaning towards creating a faceless channel, requires a keen understanding of the landscape you're about to navigate. It's not just about figuring out what content you want to produce but understanding who's already out there doing something similar, and how you can carve out your unique space. Let's break it down.

First off, it's crucial to take stock of your competition. This isn't just about knowing who the big players are. It's about understanding what they're doing right, what gaps they might be leaving open, and how their audience interacts with their content. Dive deep into their channels. Look at their most popular videos. What themes do you notice? Is there a particular style or approach that seems to resonate with their audience?

But here's where it gets interesting. While analyzing these successful channels, ask yourself: what aren't they covering? Sometimes, the gold isn't in following exactly what they're doing but in identifying the voids within their content spectrum. This is where opportunities lie for new creators. Maybe there's a subtopic they touched on only briefly that you can expand into a whole series. Perhaps there's an angle or perspective they've completely missed.

Next, let's talk about evaluating opportunities. This isn't just a creative endeavor; it's a strategic one. You need to look at market trends, search volumes, and audience demand. Tools like Google Trends and YouTube's own search bar can be incredibly revealing. Type in the broad topics related to your niche and see what suggestions pop up. These are clues to what people are interested in but might not be getting enough of.

Consider the demographics of your potential audience too. Different age groups, cultural backgrounds, and personal interests can drastically affect what kind of content is sought after. What's missing for them? Can you deliver it in a way that's both engaging and unique?

Now, don't get overwhelmed by the competition. Remember, every successful channel started from zero at one point. They identified their niche, found their voice, and built their community. You're on the same journey. Their success doesn't preclude yours. In fact, it highlights the potential that's out there. The key is in differentiating yourself.

How do you do that? Start by defining your unique value proposition. What makes your channel different? Is it your voiceover style, your approach to storytelling, the unique insights you bring, or the way you edit your videos? Pinpointing this can help guide your content creation process and ensure that even if you're entering a crowded niche, you have that special something that sets you apart.

Collaboration is another powerful tool in your kit. Joining forces with other creators, even those who might seem like competitors, can open up your channel to wider audiences. It's a win-win. You get exposed to their viewers, and they get exposed to yours. Look for collaboration opportunities that feel natural and beneficial to both parties.

Feedback is gold. Pay close attention to the comments and interactions on both your channel and others in your niche. What are viewers asking for? What complaints or suggestions do they have? This direct line to your audience is invaluable for tweaking your strategy and ensuring that your content remains relevant and sought-after.

Embrace adaptability. The digital landscape changes rapidly, and so do viewer preferences. Being willing to pivot your content strategy based on feedback and trends is vital. Maybe you start out focused on one particular sub-niche, but discover another related area that your audience is hungry for. Don't be afraid to explore new directions.

Experimentation is key. Not every video you post will be a hit, and that's okay. Each one is a learning opportunity. Try different video formats, lengths, and styles. Analyze what works and what doesn't. Over time, you'll refine your approach and develop a strong sense of what resonates with your audience.

Remember, patience is part of the process. Building a successful faceless YouTube channel doesn't happen overnight. It takes consistent effort, strategic planning, and a willingness to learn and adapt. But the opportunities are out there. If you're keenly observing the landscape, understanding your competition, and identifying those gaps in the market, you're laying the groundwork for a channel that not only succeeds but thrives.

Lastly, never underestimate the power of your own unique perspective. Even in a crowded niche, your individual experiences, insights, and creativity can bring something entirely new to the table. Keep honing your voice and your vision. The YouTube universe is vast, and there's room for channels that break the mold and offer something truly special.

As you embark on this journey, keep these principles in mind. Evaluating competition and opportunities isn't a one-time task but an ongoing part of your growth as a creator. Stay curious, stay nimble, and most importantly, stay true to what drives you. The path might not always be straightforward, but with the right approach, your faceless YouTube channel can reach heights you've only imagined.

Case Studies: Successful Faceless Channels in Different Niches

Finding your niche is like digging for gold; once you hit a seam, everything else falls into place. To light up that path, let's dip into some remarkable case studies of faceless channels that have carved their unique spaces across various niches. These examples aren't just success stories - they're a blueprint for how you can replicate their achievements in your own way.

First up is a channel that dives deep into the mysteries of our world - think unexplained phenomena and historical enigmas. Without showing a single face, they've amassed millions of views by narrating captivating stories, all while leveraging high-quality stock footage and gripping voiceovers. The key takeaway here? Your passion and storytelling skills can turn even the most obscure topics into viewer magnets.

Next, consider the animation and explainer video niche. A certain channel shines by breaking down complex ideas into digestible, animated sequences. They tackle everything from science to philosophy without any on-screen presence. The lesson here is straightforward - complex information, when presented simply and creatively, can build a massive audience.

Moving on to the world of finance and investment, there's a channel that has perfected the art of faceless content. Through comprehensive voiceovers and visuals, including charts and bullet points, they make financial education accessible and interesting. If you have expertise in a particular field, sharing your knowledge could be your golden ticket to success.

In the fitness sector, a channel has reimagined workout videos by focusing on animated demonstrations and voice-guided routines. They've found a unique angle by eliminating the need for a fitness instructor's physical presence, which proves that niche success often lies in innovative content delivery.

Then there's the lifestyle and productivity space, where a channel has thrived by offering tips on minimalism, self-improvement, and productivity hacks through compelling voiceovers and relevant visuals. This example underscores the importance of addressing everyday challenges and aspirations, connecting with viewers on a personal level.

For those interested in cooking and recipes, there's a faceless channel that's stirring up success. By focusing solely on the ingredients and the cooking process, their videos are both informative and immensely satisfying to watch. This highlights that sometimes, simplicity coupled with high-quality production can outshine on-camera presence.

In the realm of storytelling and narration, some channels have leveraged the power of voice to bring stories to life. Whether it's horror narratives or heartwarming tales, these channels captivate listeners with only their voice, proving that sometimes, what we hear is just as impactful as what we see.

Moving to a different beat, the music compilation niche thrives with faceless channels that curate and share music tracks across various moods and genres. Without any need for a visual persona, these channels have become go-to places for music lovers, showing how curating existing content can also carve out a niche.

Then, there's the educational space where channels have taken complex subjects like mathematics, physics, and coding, and broken them down into comprehensive, easy-to-follow tutorials. By removing the instructor's face from the equation, they've made the content timeless and focused solely on the learning experience.

In the travel and adventure niche, some channels have embraced the beauty of the world without any presenter in sight. Through stunning drone footage and captivating voiceovers, they take viewers on journeys to breathtaking destinations, proving that you don't need to be in front of the camera to inspire wanderlust.

Lastly, in the realm of crafts and DIY, faceless channels are making a huge impact by focusing purely on the creation process. From woodworking to painting, these channels mesmerize viewers with their hands-on demonstrations, showing that skills and creativity can speak louder than words.

These case studies demonstrate that regardless of your chosen niche, success is achievable without stepping in front of the camera. What binds these varied examples is clear, value-driven content that resonates with their specific audience. They've understood their viewers' needs and preferences, tailored their content accordingly, and found innovative ways to present traditional topics.

To emulate their success, start by pinpointing your passion and expertise. Lean into your unique skills and consider how you can deliver content that stands out. Remember, the secret sauce to a successful faceless YouTube channel lies in your ability to tell compelling stories, provide value, and engage your audience without ever showing your face.

So, as you brainstorm and plan your faceless YouTube channel, draw inspiration from these diverse niches and success stories. With creativity, dedication, and a focus on quality content, you too can build a flourishing channel that captivates and educates, all while generating passive income in the process. Let these examples light your path, and remember, the only limit is your imagination.

Chapter 2

Crafting Your Strategy

After zeroing in on the perfect niche, it's time to lay down the master plan! Crafting your strategy is like drawing the map for your treasure hunt. Without it, you're just wandering in the vast world of YouTube, hoping to stumble upon success. This chapter revolves around sketching that map with precision, standing on the shoulders of giants who've navigated these waters before us. We start by setting clear, achievable goals and objectives because, let's face it, shooting in the dark is no way to hit your target. We're talking about goals that stretch you but are as attainable as that morning coffee you can't live without. Next up, we'll dive into the nitty-gritty of developing a content calendar and schedule. Think of it as organizing a party where each video is a guest bringing its unique flavor to the table.

But who's coming to this party? That's where defining your target audience comes in. Imagine crafting content that resonates so deeply with your viewers that they can't help but hit subscribe and ding that notification bell. We'll get into the weeds of creating a unique value proposition too, because being another face in the crowd isn't our goal. We aim to stand out so much that missing out on your content would feel like missing the final episode of their favorite series. By the end of this chapter, you'll have a blueprint in hand, ready to build an empire of faceless YouTube channels that doesn't just aimlessly gather views but achieves real, tangible goals. Let's set the stage for a journey towards not just creating content, but making an impact and generating passive income while we're at it.

Setting Clear Goals and Objectives

So, you've decided to embark on the journey of creating a faceless YouTube channel. That's awesome! But let's get one thing straight from the get-go: without setting clear goals and objectives, you might as well be shooting in the dark. Goals are the blueprint for your channel's success. They give you a sense of direction and help measure how well you're doing. This chapter is all about helping you set those winning objectives to ensure your faceless YouTube channel doesn't just float aimlessly in the vast sea of content.

First thing's first, let's talk about the 'why.' Ask yourself, 'Why am I starting this channel?' This isn't just some deep philosophical question; it's the cornerstone of your strategy. Maybe you're looking to generate a passive income, or perhaps you want to educate or entertain. Whatever it is, pinning down your 'why' will guide every decision you make from here on out.

Once you've got your 'why,' it's time to drill down into the specifics. This means setting SMART goals – Specific, Measurable, Achievable, Relevant, and Time-bound. For example, don't just say you want to 'make money' from your channel. Instead, aim for something like, 'Generate $1,000 per month from ad revenue within one year.' See how much clearer that second goal is?

Here's a pro tip: write your goals down. There's something about putting pen to paper that makes things feel more real. Plus, it'll be handy to have your goals visible as a constant reminder of what you're working towards.

Now, let's dive a little deeper into the types of goals you might set. These can range from subscriber counts, to income targets, to engagement rates like comments and likes. But remember, while subscribers might seem like the be-all and end-all, engagement is the true king. Engaged viewers are more likely to stick around, share your content, and ultimately, contribute to your channel's success.

Consider also setting some objectives around the content itself. Aim to produce a certain number of videos within a timeframe or commit to mastering a new editing skill. Creating great content is what will keep viewers coming back for more, after all.

Then there's the matter of growth milestones. It's essential to celebrate the small wins on your way to the top. Maybe your first goal is to hit 100 subscribers. When you reach that, take a moment to acknowledge your progress before setting your sights on the next target, like 1,000 subscribers. These milestones are motivational checkpoints that keep you pushing forward.

An essential part of goal setting is also being realistic. It's great to aim high, but setting unattainable objectives can be a fast track to burnout and disappointment. Be honest with yourself about what you can achieve with the resources and time you have.

To stay on track, regular check-ins on your progress are a must. Schedule a monthly review of your goals and assess where you're at. What's working? What isn't? And be prepared to pivot if necessary. Adaptability can be just as important as sticking to a plan.

Leveraging analytics will be a game-changer in this respect. Platforms like YouTube Studio provide a wealth of data that can help you understand how your content is performing. Use this data to refine your strategy and ensure you're always moving in the right direction.

Collaboration can also play a pivotal role in achieving your goals. Connecting with other creators, even if they're not in your exact niche, can provide valuable insights and opportunities for cross-promotion.

And hey, while we're talking goals, let's not forget about the importance of setting personal development objectives too. Whether it's improving your voiceover skills or getting better at scripting, focusing on self-improvement will directly impact the quality of your content.

Finally, it's critical to remember that goals should inspire and motivate you, not create undue stress. It's okay to adjust your objectives if they're no longer serving you or if you find a new direction you're passionate about. The journey of building a successful faceless YouTube channel is a marathon, not a sprint.

So, to wrap this up: setting clear, actionable, and achievable goals is the foundation of any successful YouTube channel. Take the time to craft these goals thoughtfully, and you'll give yourself a roadmap to success. Remember, every big achievement starts with the decision to try. So set those goals, take that first step, and don't look back. Your YouTube journey is just beginning, and the possibilities are endless.

Developing a Content Calendar and Schedule

Once you've honed in on your strategy, it's time to talk about one of the most crucial parts of your content plan: the content calendar and schedule. Think of your content calendar as your roadmap to success. It's not just about knowing what you're going to post, but also when and how often. Consistency is key on YouTube, and a well-thought-out calendar helps you stay on track, meet your goals, and keep your audience engaged and coming back for more.

First off, let's break down what a content calendar should include. At a minimum, it needs your post dates, topics, and any key themes you're working with. Some creators like to get more detailed, adding in notes about target keywords, potential collaborations, and specific call-to-actions for each video. Whether you keep it simple or go in-depth is up to you, but remember, the goal is to make your life easier, not more complicated.

The rhythm of your posting schedule is next. How often should you post? Well, there's no one-size-fits-all answer, but consistency is your friend. Whether it's once a week, twice a week, or daily, pick a pace you can sustain. It's better to start with a manageable schedule and scale up than to burn out trying to do too much, too soon.

Consider your niche and your audience. Some niches, like news or current events, might demand more frequent updates. Others, like in-depth tutorials or storytelling, might benefit from a slightly less frequent, but more polished, approach. Understanding your audience's expectations can help tailor your schedule to fit both their desires and your capabilities.

Utilizing tools can make scheduling a breeze. There's a plethora of content calendar apps and software out there, from simple spreadsheets to comprehensive programs like Trello, Asana, or Later. These tools can help you visualize your schedule, set reminders for production milestones, and track your progress. The best part? Many have free versions that are perfect for getting started.

Batching content is another game-changer. Instead of scrambling to create each video one at a time, try producing multiple videos in one go. This can help you work more efficiently and free up time to focus on other aspects of your channel, like engaging with your community or brainstorming new content ideas.

Flexibility is crucial. Your content calendar isn't set in stone. Life happens, trends pop up, and feedback might steer you in new directions. While it's essential to stick to your schedule as much as possible, don't be afraid to adjust your plan to accommodate new ideas or opportunities that come your way.

Don't overlook holidays and events. Planning content around key dates, whether it's Christmas, Halloween, or international days related to your niche, can boost engagement and relevance. Make note of these dates in your calendar and plan your content accordingly, whether it's a special one-off video or a themed series leading up to the event.

Remember, the goal is sustainable growth. It's tempting to look at successful channels and think you need to match their output from day one. Focus on building a schedule that allows you to produce quality content consistently without sacrificing your well-being. Over time, as you streamline your workflow and understand your audience better, you can adjust your frequency and production values.

Another key element is strategic planning. While it's important to stay flexible, having a long-term view of your content can help you align your videos with your overall channel goals. Think seasons, not just individual episodes. Planning content in "seasons" or series can help keep your audience hooked and looking forward to what's next.

Audit and adapt. Make it a habit to regularly review your content calendar's effectiveness. Which videos are hitting the mark? Which ones aren't? Use data from YouTube Analytics to guide your adjustments. Pay attention to which posting times yield the highest engagement and tweak your schedule accordingly.

Including evergreen content in your calendar ensures your channel has a stable base. These are videos that remain relevant long after publication, helping attract viewers over time. Blending these with trending topics gives your channel both stability and immediacy, a combination that can help build sustained growth.

Collaborations can be a boon for your content calendar. Planning collaborations with other creators can spice up your content, introduce your channel to new audiences, and keep your existing viewers excited. Be sure to plan these well in advance, as coordinating with others can add complexity to your schedule.

Lastly, make sure your content calendar is visible and accessible. Whether it's a physical planner on your desk or a digital one on your devices, having easy access to your plan helps keep everything in perspective. It serves as a constant reminder of what you've committed to and what you're working towards.

Developing a content calendar and schedule is an ongoing process of trial and learning. It's about finding what works best for you and your channel, then refining and improving over time. With consistency, flexibility, and a bit of creativity, your content calendar will be a powerful tool in building and maintaining a successful faceless YouTube channel.

Defining Your Target Audience

Jumping right in from setting our sights on clear goals and whipping up a robust content calendar, there's a critical piece of the puzzle we can't afford to overlook — identifying who our content is for. This isn't about throwing videos into the digital universe and hoping they stick. It's about knowing the faces behind the screens, the real people clicking on our content. So, let's dive deep into defining your target audience, a step that could well be the linchpin in the success of your faceless YouTube channel.

First things first, understanding your target audience means getting inside their heads. What are their interests? Their problems? Their browsing habits? You see, it's not just about demographics like age, location, or gender, though those are important. It's more about psychographics: values, attitudes, and lifestyle. This nuanced understanding of your audience guides everything from the tone of your videos to the topics you choose.

Now, you might be thinking, "But my content could appeal to everyone!" And while broad appeal is great, a jack-of-all-trades is a master of none. Carving out a niche audience might seem limiting, but it actually allows you to speak directly to the viewers most likely to engage with your content, subscribe, and keep coming back for more.

But how do you start narrowing down this audience? Start with your content's subject matter. Who would benefit most from your videos? If you're creating cooking tutorials without showing your face, are you aiming for busy professionals looking for quick meals, or health-conscious individuals trying to prep meals in advance? Each group requires a different approach, even if the overarching theme is similar.

And don't forget about competitor analysis. Checking out successful channels in your niche can offer insights into who their videos are resonating with. Look at their most popular videos, read the comments, and see who's engaging with their content. This isn't about copying what they're doing but rather understanding the existing audience landscape within your niche.

Engagement is another key piece of the puzzle. Pay attention to the engagement on your own videos as well as on competitors'. Which videos get the most likes, comments, or shares? This feedback is invaluable and direct from the audience you're trying to target. They're telling you what they like, what they don't, and, if you're paying attention, what they wish to see more of.

You also want to think about your content's searchability. What keywords are your potential viewers using? Tools like Google's Keyword Planner and YouTube's Search Suggest feature can offer a treasure trove of insight into what your target audience is looking for. This can help you not only to fine-tune your content but also to optimize it for discovery.

Creating personae can be immensely helpful too. This means crafting detailed profiles for different segments of your potential audience. What's a day in their life like? What challenges do they face, and how can your content help? These personae become your go-to guides whenever you're planning new content or tweaking your strategy.

A big mistake many new creators make is trying to appeal to their audience solely based on assumption or gut feeling. While intuition plays a role, data should drive your decisions. YouTube Analytics is a goldmine for understanding who's watching your videos, how they found them, and what keeps them engaged. Use this data to refine your approach over time continually.

Another crucial factor is to listen to your audience actively. This means not just reading comments but encouraging feedback, asking questions, and maybe even conducting surveys. The more you engage, the better you'll understand what makes your audience tick. This two-way conversation can't be underestimated; it's the foundation of a community, not just an audience.

Consider, too, the evolving nature of your audience. As your channel grows, so too will your audience. They might evolve in terms of demographics, interests, and preferences. It's important to revisit and possibly redefine your target audience as you scale. This keeps your content relevant and engaging for your viewers, old and new.

Let's not forget about the psychological aspect. The success of your content isn't just about what it offers practically but also how it makes your audience feel. Are you inspiring them? Educating them? Entertaining them? The emotional takeaway is a huge part of why viewers keep coming back.

Finally, integrating your audience's preferences with your passion is crucial. It's one thing to identify a target audience; it's another to create content for them that you're also passionate about. This genuine enthusiasm for your topic shines through and is infectious. It builds a deeper connection with your audience and fosters a loyal community around your channel.

Defining your target audience is an ongoing process. It's about combining art with science: the art of understanding human nature and the science of analyzing data. So take these insights, start putting them into practice, and remember that the better you know your audience, the more effectively you can reach them, engage them, and turn them into loyal followers of your faceless YouTube channel. Here's to crafting content that connects and resonates, one video at a time.

Creating a Unique Value Proposition

So you've set your sights on launching a faceless YouTube channel. You know your niche, you've got an eye on your target audience, and you're buzzing with content ideas. But here's something pivotal that can't be overlooked: your unique value proposition (UVP). This isn't just marketing jargon; it's the backbone of your channel's identity. Let's dive deep into what makes a compelling UVP and how it can set you apart in the boundless ocean of content creators.

First off, understanding what a UVP actually is can be a game-changer. Think of it like this: your UVP clearly articulates why someone should watch your videos instead of the millions of other options available. It's that special sauce, your channel's signature flavor that makes viewers choose you.

To craft your UVP, start with pinpointing what makes your channel unique. Is it your approach to storytelling? Your video quality? Maybe it's the way you break down complex ideas into digestible, engaging content. Whatever it is, it needs to resonate with your intended audience.

Consider the needs and wants of your target viewers. What issues are they facing? What are they searching for on YouTube, and how can your channel provide that in a way no one else does? This is where understanding your audience really pays off, allowing you to tailor your UVP to meet their specific desires.

Once you have a grasp on what sets you apart, it's time to distill this down into a clear, concise statement. Your UVP shouldn't be a paragraph; it needs to be a punchy one-liner or two that instantly communicates your channel's essence. And this goes beyond just your content—it's about the experience viewers will have on your channel.

But crafting your UVP isn't a one-and-done deal. It's a living, breathing statement that can evolve. As you develop your channel and delve deeper into your niche, you may find new aspects of your content that viewers are drawn to. Stay flexible and be willing to revise your UVP as you grow.

Integrating your UVP into everything you do is crucial. It should shine through in your video titles, your descriptions, your channel art, and even in the way you interact with your viewers. Consistency here will reinforce your unique value and help build a loyal viewer base.

Now, let's not forget about the competitive landscape. Analyzing your competition is a great way to refine your UVP. See what others in your niche are offering and think about how you can do it differently, or better. This could be the quality of your content, unique perspectives on topics, or even the community you build around your channel.

Implementing your UVP means more than just stating it; it requires action. Craft content that consistently delivers on the promise of your unique value. Each video should be a piece of evidence that substantiates your UVP, compelling viewers to stick around and see what's next.

Feedback is your best friend when it comes to fine-tuning your UVP. Engage with your audience, ask for their opinions, and listen to their needs. Their responses can offer invaluable insights into how your UVP is perceived and areas where it might be enhanced.

In a sea of content, being forgettable is a fate worse than having a small audience. Your UVP is your beacon, guiding viewers to your channel. It's about being remembered, respected, and revisited. That kind of impact is what turns a casual viewer into a devoted fan.

Emotional connections can't be understated here. People watch and subscribe to channels because of how they make them feel. Whether you're inspiring, educating, or entertaining, your UVP should include an emotional component that hooks viewers and keeps them coming back for more.

Success on YouTube isn't just about having high-quality content; it's about having content that's unequivocally yours. By creating and implementing a powerful UVP, you ensure that your channel isn't just another drop in the digital ocean but a lighthouse - bright, inviting, and impossible to ignore.

Remember, your UVP also sets the stage for monetization down the road. Advertisers, sponsors, and partners are looking for channels that stand out, offering something truly unique to their audience. A strong UVP makes you far more attractive to potential collaborators and sponsors, paving the way for diverse revenue streams.

In wrapping up, creating a unique value proposition might seem like a tall order, but it's within your reach. Reflect on what makes your channel special, understand your audience deeply, craft your UVP with clarity and conviction, and infuse it into every aspect of your channel. Do this, and you're not just making videos; you're building a brand that resonates, impacts, and grows. Let your unique light shine bright and watch as the world gathers to bask in its glow.

Chapter 3

Setting Up Your Channel

Now that you've honed in on your niche and strategized your path forward, it's time to roll up your sleeves for the real action: setting up your channel. Think of this phase as laying down the bricks for your digital empire on YouTube. First off, selecting a channel name isn't just about being catchy; it's about encapsulating what you're all about while being easy to remember. It's like choosing a name for a rock band, but instead of music, you're delivering content. Next, dive into the world of visual appeal with your channel banner and logo, which are not just accessories but the face of your brand. These elements need to scream 'click me' to anyone who stumbles upon your channel.

But don't just stop at looks; a powerful channel description ties everything together, telling your audience who you are, what you do, and why they should care in a few concise sentences. Think of it as your elevator pitch to the world. And since YouTube is a playground for content, organizing your videos into optimized playlists can keep viewers hooked and wanting more. Each of these steps is a piece in the puzzle of building a successful faceless YouTube channel that doesn't just attract viewers but engages and retains them, setting you on the path to making that sweet passive income. So, let's get into the nitty-gritty and set you up for success.

Choosing a Memorable Channel Name

So, you've carved out your niche, sketched out your strategy, and now you're standing at the exciting threshold of bringing your faceless YouTube channel to life. The first step? Picking a channel name that sticks. This isn't just about slapping a cool label on your creation; it's about setting the tone, character, and identity of your channel right from the get-go.

Think of your channel name as the front door to your world. It needs to be welcoming, intriguing, and, most importantly, memorable. A great channel name not only captures the essence of your content but also etches itself into the minds of viewers, encouraging them to click, revisit, and subscribe.

You might wonder, "What makes a channel name 'memorable'?" The answer lies in its simplicity, relevance, and uniqueness. A simple name is easy to remember and pronounce. When it's relevant, it gives potential viewers a hint of what to expect, aligning with their interests. Uniqueness, on the other hand, ensures that your channel stands out in a sea of content, offering something that can't be found elsewhere.

Brainstorming can be your best friend or your worst enemy in this phase. Start by jotting down words, phrases, or concepts that best describe your channel's essence. Don't hold back—creativity here is everything. Use tools like thesauruses or online name generators to spice things up but take the results with a grain of salt. Your goal isn't to pick a random name but to find inspiration that aligns with your vision.

Once you have a list, start playing around with combinations, keeping in mind the factors of simplicity, relevance, and uniqueness. It's like piecing together a puzzle where the final image is your channel's identity. Ask yourself, "Would a new viewer grasp what my channel is about at a glance?" If the answer is a resounding "Yes," you're on the right path.

Feedback is gold during this stage. Share your top choices with friends, family, or even potential viewers if you have access to your target audience. Their insights can highlight perspectives you might have missed and help refine your selection. Remember, what makes sense to you might not resonate with others in the same way.

Consider the future scalability of your channel name. Your channel might evolve, branching out into sub-niches or entirely new directions. A name too specific might box you in, limiting growth opportunities. Aim for a balance between specificity and flexibility to keep doors open for future expansion.

Check for availability and uniqueness across not just YouTube, but all social media platforms and the web. A unique name reduces confusion and builds a cohesive brand identity across the internet. Securing a matching domain and social media handles ideally should be part of your naming process, ensuring you own your channel's identity everywhere.

Don't forget about the legalities. Ensure your chosen name doesn't infringe on trademarks or copyrights. This might seem like a minor detail now, but it can spare you from potential headaches and legal issues down the road.

At this point, you might have a couple of frontrunners in your naming race. Sit with them for a while. Sometimes, a name's appeal can grow or fade over time. If a name still feels right after a period of contemplation, chances are you've struck gold.

Finally, when you've selected that perfect name, it's time to embrace it fully. Start infusing it into every piece of your channel - your logo, banner, intro, outro, and anywhere else your brand appears.

Consistency is key in branding, and it starts with a name that carries through every aspect of your channel.

In the end, remember that your channel name is just the beginning. It sets the stage, but it's the quality of your content that will keep viewers coming back. A fantastic name paired with equally fantastic content? Now that's a recipe for success.

So, take a deep breath and dive into the creative process of naming your channel. It's not just a task; it's the first step in your journey to creating a memorable, impactful faceless YouTube channel that stands the test of time. Your name is your banner in the digital sky, make it fly high.

Motivation and inspiration are what we aim for, but action is what gets us across the finish line. Choosing a channel name isn't just about making a decision; it's about making a statement. It's about declaring, "Here I am, world. Ready or not, here I come." And with the right name, the world will indeed be ready to welcome your channel with open arms and eager eyes. So, let the brainstorming commence, and may your channel name be the beacon that guides viewers your way.

Designing an Engaging Channel Banner and Logo

So you've got your channel name down, and it's time to bring it to life with some visual pop! This stage is critical; your channel's banner and logo are the first things viewers will notice when they land on your page. Think of them as your channel's handshake or first impression. If executed well, they'll tell your audience exactly what your faceless YouTube channel is all about without a single word being spoken.

Let's dive into the logo first. This little graphic is more than just a picture; it's the symbol of your brand's identity. When someone sees it in their subscription box or on social media, it should instantly click that it's you. For faceless channels, where you don't rely on a personal brand, your logo has to work even harder to convey your niche and vibe. Keep it simple but memorable. Use colors and shapes that reflect your channel's mood. If you're all about relaxation and meditation, soft tones and fluid shapes could work wonders. Meanwhile, a tech channel could benefit from sharper lines and a more dynamic color scheme.

Moving on to the channel banner, this is where you can afford to be a bit more elaborate. This space is your billboard. It's where you can share a bit more about what your channel offers. Include your upload schedule, a snappy tagline, and maybe a few keywords that sum up your content. Visual consistency between your logo and banner is key. They should complement each other, creating a cohesive look that reinforces your brand.

When it comes to actually designing these elements, you don't need to be a Photoshop expert. Tools like Canva offer fantastic templates that you can customize to suit your channel's needs. But, the most important tip here is to always keep your audience in mind. Your designs should appeal to them, using visuals and language that resonate with their preferences and expectations.

Another aspect to consider is responsiveness. Your banner, in particular, will be viewed across different devices, from the big screens of desktops to the compact screens of smartphones. Make sure your important information (like your channel name and tagline) is centralized and visible even on smaller screens. YouTube provides a handy template for designing channel art that keeps these variations in mind. Don't forget to utilize it!

Now, let's talk about iteration. You're not carving these designs into stone; they can — and should — evolve with your channel. As you better understand your audience or perhaps shift your content slightly, your banner and logo can be updated to reflect these changes. This keeps your channel looking fresh and aligned with your current content strategy.

Feedback is your friend here. Don't be shy to ask your audience what they think of your channel's look. You might find valuable insights that you hadn't considered. Polls in your community tab or on social media can be a great way to get feedback directly from those who matter most — your viewers.

Avoid the temptation to cram too much into your banner or logo. Clarity trumps complexity every time. You want anyone who glances at your channel to immediately understand what they can expect. If it's too busy or unclear, you risk losing their interest before they've even watched a video.

Remember, your faceless channel thrives on its content, but it's the visual branding that will make someone stop and look initially. Think of your favorite brands and what makes their visual identity stand out to you. Is it the color scheme? The simplicity? The clever use of space? Drawing inspiration from successful brands (even those outside of YouTube) can spark ideas for your own channel's design strategy.

Color psychology isn't just marketing jargon; it's a real tool you can use to your advantage. Different colors evoke different feelings and actions. For example, blue often instills a sense of trust and reliability, while yellow can make people feel happy and energetic. Consider the emotional impact of your color choices on your logo and banner design.

Investing time in creating or refreshing your channel's visual identity can seem like a chore, but it's an essential step in setting up a successful faceless YouTube channel. Your logo and banner are more than just decorations; they're strategic tools that can help attract and retain viewers.

Finally, let's not overlook the importance of alignment with your content. Your banner and logo should be a promise of the value your videos intend to deliver. If your channel's focus is on providing detailed analysis on stock market trends, a whimsical and overly colorful design might confuse your audience. Conversely, a channel dedicated to kids' educational content won't do well with a muted, minimalist logo. Every element of your design should align with the expectations your content sets.

Creating an engaging channel banner and logo is a blend of art and science. It's about understanding your audience, being aware of design principles, and not being afraid to tweak and refine as you go. Keep it simple, make it memorable, and ensure it aligns with your content for the best results. With these tools in your creator toolbox, you're setting up a solid foundation for your faceless YouTube channel's visual identity.

Remember, the journey of a thousand subscribers begins with a single click, and that click is much more likely if your channel visually invites it. So take your time, experiment with designs, and don't hesitate to evolve your visuals as your channel grows. This is just one step in building a successful faceless YouTube channel, but it's a crucial one. Visual consistency and appeal can make all the difference in converting a passerby into a loyal viewer.

Writing a Compelling Channel Description

Imagine walking into a party and not knowing anyone there. You'd look for someone approachable, someone who seems interesting and friendly, right? Similarly, when viewers stumble upon your channel, the first thing they'll look for, after glancing at your content, is your channel description. This small yet powerful section is your prime real estate to make a lasting impression, to tell viewers who you are, what your channel offers, and why they should stick around.

Now, I know what you're thinking. "But I'm not a writer!" Don't worry. Crafting a compelling channel description isn't about showcasing fancy writing skills. It's about communication. You're clarifying to potential subscribers why your faceless YouTube channel is worth their time. Here's how you can nail it.

Firstly, start with clarity. Your channel's description needs to cut through the noise. Begin with a clear, concise statement of what viewers can expect. This doesn't mean rattling off a list of video topics. Instead, convey the value your channel adds: does it solve a problem, entertain, educate, or inspire? For instance, "Unlock the secrets of passive income with our easy, step-by-step financial guides."

Inject personality. Remember, YouTube is a social platform. People crave connections, even with faceless channels. Sprinkle some personality into your description. Whether your tone is witty, inspirational, or downright quirky, make sure it shines through. This personal touch can turn a mundane description into an engaging invitation to your world.

Keywords are your best friend for SEO, but they're also crucial in your description. Weave relevant keywords naturally into your prose to boost your channel's visibility. However, avoid overstuffing; the primary goal is to engage real people, not just search algorithms.

Highlight what makes you unique. With millions of channels out there, uniqueness is key to standing out. Pinpoint what sets your channel apart and spotlight it in your description. Is it your unparalleled insights, your innovative presentation style, or perhaps the way you simplify complex topics? Whatever it is, make it known.

Don't forget the call to action (CTA). Guide your audience on what to do next — subscribe, visit your website, follow you on social media. A simple, direct CTA can significantly increase engagement rates.

Utilize storytelling. Even in the compact space of a channel description, storytelling can be powerful. Share a snippet of your journey or mission to make your channel relatable and memorable.

"Driven by a passion to empower aspiring entrepreneurs, we share tools and strategies to build your dream business."

Make updating a habit. Your channel will evolve, and so should your description. Periodically review and tweak it to ensure it reflects the latest about your channel. An out-of-date description can mislead or turn off potential subscribers.

Consider accessibility. Use simple, clear language that's easy to understand. Not only does this make your channel more inclusive, but it also caters to a wider audience, maximizing your reach.

Include social proof. If you've hit impressive milestones, been featured in notable publications, or collaborated with well-known brands or creators, mention it. This builds credibility and trust among viewers.

Format for readability. A colossal block of text is daunting. Break up your description into digestible chunks using spacing and bullet points if necessary. This improves the overall readability and allows viewers to quickly grasp your channel's essence.

Envision your ideal viewer and speak directly to them. By tailoring your language and tone to match your target audience, you create a sense of belonging and community right from the start.

Show some love for your subscribers. Acknowledge their support and express appreciation in your description. A simple "Thank you for being part of our journey" goes a long way in fostering a loyal community.

Lastly, be patient and experiment. Finding the perfect blend of information, personality, and keywords might take a few tries. Monitor how small changes affect your channel's growth and engagement, and don't be afraid to tweak your description accordingly.

In essence, your channel description is more than just a summary of your content — it's a powerful tool to attract and retain viewers, encapsulate your brand, and set the stage for your YouTube growth journey. Take the time to craft it well, and it will pay dividends in building a successful, faceless YouTube channel that generates passive income and leaves a lasting impact.

Optimizing Playlists for Better Viewer Retention

Think of your YouTube channel as a garden. Your videos are the plants, flourishing with engaging content. But to guide your visitors through the garden, you need paths. Playlists are these paths, guiding viewers from one video to the next, keeping them engaged and on your channel longer. It's not just about having content; it's about serving it up in a way that makes your audience stick around. Let's dive into how optimizing your playlists can significantly enhance viewer retention.

First up, consider the structure of your playlists. Many creators make the mistake of throwing videos together without much thought. However, a curated approach is key. Arrange your videos in a sequence that tells a story or logically progresses. This could mean grouping similar topics together or arranging tutorials in a step-by-step guide. By doing this, you're not only making your content more accessible but also encouraging viewers to binge-watch your channel.

Customizing playlist titles and descriptions also plays a pivotal role. Use keywords not just for SEO, but to clearly describe what viewers can expect from the playlist. This clarity can be the difference between someone clicking on your playlist or scrolling past. Think of each playlist as its own mini-channel. Make it compelling, make it clear, and watch as it works wonders for your viewer retention rates.

Don't underestimate the importance of the first video in your playlist. This video acts as the hook. If it's engaging and offers value, chances are viewers will stick around for more. Select a strong opener that represents the playlist well and entices viewers to keep watching. A strong start can lead to a strong finish.

Engagement doesn't stop with creating playlists. You need to actively promote them. Feature your playlists in video descriptions, pin them in comments, or even mention them in your videos. Treat your playlists like they're as important as individual videos because, in many ways, they are. They represent another layer of your content strategy that can significantly boost retention time.

Updating your playlists regularly is another crucial step. As your channel grows and evolves, so should your playlists. Add new videos, rearrange existing ones to keep the playlists fresh and relevant. This not only helps with retention but also signals to YouTube that your channel is active and thriving, which can help with overall visibility.

Remember, the aim here is to keep the viewer's journey smooth and engaging. Another helpful tip is to check the "autoplay next video" feature for your playlists. This encourages continuous play, which can keep viewers on your channel for longer periods.

Analytics should become your best friend. Use YouTube's Analytics tool to monitor how your playlists are performing. Look at metrics like average watch time, drop-off points, and engagement rates. These insights can help you optimize your playlists even further, tweaking them based on what your audience enjoys the most.

Consider the narrative arc when arranging your playlist. Even if your videos are not straightforward stories, you can still arrange them in a way that builds up interest over time. Start with the basics or introductory topics and gradually move towards more in-depth content. This gradual increase in complexity can keep viewers intrigued and motivated to follow through the entire playlist.

Collaborations can also enhance your playlists. If you're working with other creators, creating shared playlists can expose your content to a broader audience. It's a win-win: their viewers get introduced to your content, and your viewers discover new creators they might enjoy.

Cross-promotion between playlists is another tactic. Once a viewer has completed a playlist, guide them to another of your playlists. This can be done through end screens and cards strategically placed at the end of the last video in a playlist. It's like telling your viewers, "If you enjoyed this, you're going to love what's next."

Personalization is key. If you're addressing different segments within your audience, create playlists tailored to each segment. This level of personalization can significantly enhance viewer retention as it caters to the specific interests of your viewers, making them feel understood and valued.

Addressing viewer feedback in your playlists can be a game-changer. If your audience is asking for more content on a specific topic, create a playlist around it. This responsiveness not only boosts engagement but also creates a sense of community around your channel.

Lastly, don't forget about the aesthetics. Use visually appealing thumbnails for your playlists, just as you would for your videos. Consistency in design across your channel and playlists can significantly impact a viewer's decision to stick around. A cohesive, visually appealing channel is more likely to retain viewers than a disjointed one.

In conclusion, optimizing your playlists is not just about better organization; it's a powerful tool to enhance viewer retention and, ultimately, champion the success of your faceless YouTube channel. Treat playlists with the same care as individual videos, and they can become a significant asset in building and maintaining an engaged audience. Now, go forth and optimize. Your viewers, and your analytics, will thank you for it.

Chapter 4

Content Creation and Production

Now that your channel is all set up and looking sharp, let's dive into the heart of what makes a YouTube channel thrive: compelling content creation and efficient production processes. Crafting videos that resonate with your audience starts with mastering the art of storytelling. Engaging narratives capture attention and keep viewers coming back for more. However, a good story needs to be well scripted, especially when you're working on a faceless channel where visually engaging content and a captivating voiceover are key. To help you achieve this, we'll explore some scriptwriting and voiceover tips that will breathe life into your stories.

Finding high-quality, royalty-free media can be a puzzle in itself, but worry not! We've got some recommendations that'll make this process a breeze, ensuring your videos are as visually appealing as they are informative. Another game-changer in your content creation journey will be diving into the world of editing tools and software. Whether you're a seasoned pro or a newbie, we'll discuss options that cater to all skill levels, helping you create polished videos that stand out.

And let's not forget about building efficient production workflows. Time is money, and the more streamlined your process, the quicker you'll be able to produce content without sacrificing quality. By the end of this chapter, you'll have a toolbox full of strategies and resources to help you produce content that not only engages and entertains your audience but also sets your faceless YouTube channel up for long-term success. Let's get started on transforming your creative ideas into captivating videos that keep your viewers coming back for more.

Storytelling Techniques for Engaging Videos

Mastering the art of storytelling is pivotal in capturing and holding your audience's attention, especially when you're running a faceless YouTube channel. It's about weaving a captivating narrative that resonates with viewers, making them feel emotionally connected to the content you produce. Let's dive into the world of storytelling techniques that can elevate your videos from good to unforgettable.

Firstly, understand your audience. Every gripping story speaks directly to its listeners, addressing their curiosity, answering their questions, or solving their problems. Begin by identifying who your audience is, what they're interested in, and what kind of stories they might find compelling.

Create a strong hook right at the start. Just as a fisherman uses bait to catch fish, you need a hook to catch your viewer's attention. This could be a provocative question, an intriguing statement, or a teaser of what's to come. The goal is to get viewers to stick around and watch the video in its entirety.

Structure your content into a clear beginning, middle, and end. This classic narrative structure is universally recognized and helps in guiding your audience through the story smoothly. Start by setting the scene, introduce the main points or conflict in the middle, and wrap everything up with a satisfying conclusion.

Utilize the power of visuals. Since we're talking about video content, your storytelling isn't limited to words. Incorporate compelling visuals that complement your narrative. Whether it's engaging graphics, vivid images, or just well-thought-out text on screen, visuals can significantly enhance the storytelling experience.

Embrace the beauty of simplicity. Some of the most powerful stories are simple ones. Avoid complicating your narrative with unnecessary details. Keeping things simple ensures that your message is clear and easy to understand, which is crucial for faceless channels where visuals and voiceovers are your primary tools.

Use emotions wisely. An emotional connection can greatly boost engagement and retention. Whether you aim to inspire, entertain, educate, or provoke thought, tapping into the emotional aspect of storytelling can make your content more relatable and memorable.

Implement a consistent tone and style. This doesn't mean all your videos should look the same, but maintaining a consistent tone helps in building a recognizable brand identity. Decide whether you want your channel to be funny, inspirational, educational, or something else, and keep your storytelling in line with this tone.

Incorporate characters or mascots. Even if your channel is faceless, characters or mascots can serve as your virtual "face." They can be recurring elements in your stories, making your content more engaging and giving your channel a unique personality.

Highlight conflicts or challenges. Stories with conflicts or challenges tend to be more engaging because they introduce suspense and excitement. How you resolve these conflicts can provide valuable lessons or insights, making your content not only entertaining but also educational.

Don't underestimate the power of music. Just like in movies, the background score in your videos can play a huge role in setting the mood, building tension, or amplifying emotions. It's a subtle yet effective tool in storytelling that can greatly enhance the viewer's experience.

Engage the senses. While videos primarily appeal to the sense of sight and hearing, effective storytelling can engage other senses vicariously. Descriptive language and immersive visuals can make viewers almost "feel" the story, making the experience more vivid and engaging.

Invite viewers to imagine. Asking viewers to use their imagination can be a powerful storytelling tool. Pose hypothetical scenarios or encourage them to envision solutions to problems you're discussing. This not only makes the content interactive but also helps in deeper engagement.

End with a call to action. Every story should have a purpose, and in the world of content creation, usually, it's to inspire some form of action. Whether it's to learn more about a topic, apply a technique, or simply engage with more content, a clear call to action ties your story back to its objective.

Tell stories that matter to you. Your passion for a subject will shine through in your storytelling, making it more authentic and compelling. If you're genuinely interested or invested in what you're telling, your audience is more likely to be engaged as well.

Remember, storytelling is an art that can always be refined and improved. Experiment with different techniques, listen to your audience's feedback, and continually hone your skills. With dedication and creative flair, you can turn your faceless YouTube channel into a treasury of captivating stories that not only draw viewers in but also keep them coming back for more.

Scripting and Voiceover Tips

Jumping right into the heart of content creation, the magic often starts with scripting and the charm of voiceover. Crafting a script that not only holds but captivates your audience is an art form that, once mastered, can elevate your content to new heights. It's not just what you say; it's how you say it.

First off, let's tackle scripting. A well-structured script serves as your roadmap through the wilderness of content creation. It's tempting to wing it, especially when you're just starting out, thinking it might feel more 'natural'. However, scripting ensures your content is coherent, concise, and compelling. Think of it as your blueprint for success.

Now, how do you write a script that's both informative and engaging? Start with a clear outline. Break your video into segments: an introduction that hooks, a body that delivers the meat of your message, and a conclusion that ties everything neatly together. Use short, punchy sentences to keep energy up and avoid losing viewers to the dreaded 'click away'.

Voiceover adds another layer of engagement. The right tone can make or break your video. It's not just about having a good voice; it's about using your voice effectively. Are you narrating a dramatic documentary? A softer, more measured tone might be needed. A high-energy tech review? Then, let your excitement show through your voice. Adaptation is key.

Here's a tip that can't be stressed enough: practice, practice, practice. You might feel silly talking to yourself, but rehearsing your script can smooth out any awkward phrasing and help you find the perfect cadence. Remember, conveyance with authenticity breeds connection. Your audience can tell when you're genuinely interested in your topic, and this passion translates into captivating content.

Consider the technical side of voiceover too. Investing in a quality microphone is crucial. It doesn't have to break the bank, but clear audio is non-negotiable. Pair this with a pop filter and some basic soundproofing, and you're well on your way to professional-grade audio.

Let's talk about editing your script and audio. Be ruthless in cutting fluff. If a sentence doesn't add value, chop it. This applies to both your script and your recorded voiceover. Less is often more; the clearer and more concise your message, the more likely it is to resonate with viewers.

Utilizing a conversational tone can also bridge the gap between you and your audience. You're not delivering a lecture; you're sharing information or telling a story. Imagine you're talking to a friend. This mindset can transform your delivery from stilted to smooth.

Diversify your delivery by changing the pace and emphasizing key points. Variation keeps listeners engaged. Monotony is the enemy of retention. Paint your narrative with the dynamics of your voice, and watch the engagement levels soar.

Always remember, scripting and voiceover are deeply personal and ultimately subjective. What works for one creator might not for another. Experiment with different styles and approaches. Listen to feedback from your audience and be willing to adapt. Growth is a process of continual learning and fine-tuning.

For those of you who feel uncomfortable with your own voice or lack the equipment for high-quality recordings, consider hiring voiceover talents. The internet is teeming with talented individuals who can bring your script to life. This can add an extra layer of professionalism to your content and free up your time to focus on other aspects of creation.

Don't overlook the power of silence. Strategic pauses can be incredibly effective in highlighting important points or letting an idea sink in. In a world that's always on, a moment of silence can be surprisingly impactful.

Lastly, always end your video with a call to action. Whether it's encouraging viewers to subscribe, like, or comment, make sure your script guides them towards this goal gently but unmistakably. Your voiceover here should be compelling, inviting viewers to engage further with your content.

In conclusion, scripting and performing a voiceover are pivotal components in the world of faceless YouTube channels. They breathe life into your content, transforming raw information into stories that captivate, convince, and convert. As you embark on your journey, remember to write with clarity, speak with passion, and always aim to connect with your audience on a human level. The road to mastery is a journey of continual improvement, so embrace the process and watch as your channel grows.

So, there you have it. By honing your scripting and voiceover skills, you're not just creating videos; you're crafting experiences. Experiences that inform, entertain, and inspire. In the digital universe, where content is king, these skills are your scepter. Wield them well, and watch your kingdom expand.

Finding and Using Royalty-Free Media

Creating captivating content for your faceless YouTube channel means you'll often need high-quality media. But here's the scoop: not all creators have the budget to shoot their own footage or commission music tracks. That's where royalty-free media becomes a game-changer. Let's dive into how you can find and use royalty-free media to elevate your videos, without breaking the bank.

First up, understanding what "royalty-free" actually means is crucial. It's a type of license that allows you to use media without paying ongoing royalties. However, don't confuse it with "free." Some royalty-free content might require a one-time purchase. The beauty of royalty-free media is that it opens up a vast library of professional-grade content that's just waiting to be used in your projects.

Now, where to find this media? There are countless websites dedicated to providing royalty-free images, videos, and music. For images and video clips, websites like Pixabay and Unsplash are fantastic places to start. They offer a wide range of high-resolution media that's completely free to use. For music, explore platforms such as Epidemic Sound or YouTube's own Audio Library. They're packed with tracks for every mood and genre imaginable, making it easy for you to find the perfect background score for your videos.

However, while these resources are invaluable, it's important to read the fine print. Each platform has its own set of rules regarding attribution. Some may require you to credit the creator, while others don't. Staying informed will ensure you're using media ethically and legally, maintaining your channel's credibility.

Let's talk about customizing royalty-free media. Just because you didn't shoot a video clip yourself doesn't mean you can't make it your own. Tools like Adobe Premiere Pro or even free software like DaVinci Resolve let you tweak and transform clips, aligning them with your channel's aesthetic. This can include color grading, adding text overlays, or cutting and combining different clips to create something unique.

Music can be a little trickier. While you might not be able to alter the composition, paying attention to how it blends with your visual content is key. Timing your edits to the beat of the music adds an engaging rhythm to your videos, making them more captivating.

Now, onto integrating these media elements into your videos. The art of storytelling with royalty-free media is all about relevance and enhancement. A stunning clip of a mountain range becomes more than just a visual treat when paired with content about overcoming obstacles, for instance. Similarly, a soothing background track can complement a motivational script, adding emotional depth.

What about the technical side of things? Ensuring that the media you choose is of high quality and appropriate format is vital. HD or 4K videos make your content look professional, while the right audio format (such as WAV or MP3) ensures clear playback. Also, consider the size and aspect ratio of images and videos to avoid awkward cropping or stretching in your final edits.

Experimentation plays a big role here as well. Mixing and matching different types of royalty-free media can lead to unexpected and delightful results. It's all about finding what best suits your content and style. Don't shy away from trying out various combinations to see what resonates most with your audience.

Regularity in sourcing new royalty-free media is another key tip. Fresh content keeps your channel dynamic and engaging. Reusing the same set of clips or music tracks too often can make your videos feel stale. Set aside time regularly to explore new releases on your favorite royalty-free platforms.

Let's not forget about the potential for collaboration. Many creators of royalty-free media are open to collaborations. Reaching out for custom media might not only be more affordable than you think but also gives your channel a unique edge with original content.

In balancing the use of royalty-free media, it's essential to maintain your channel's original voice. The aim is to enhance your videos with this media, not to let them carry the entire content. Your narrative and message should always be at the forefront, with the media serving as a powerful tool to amplify it.

So, what's the bottom line? Leveraging royalty-free media in your faceless YouTube channel can dramatically up your content game. It allows you to produce high-quality, engaging videos consistently and cost-effectively. Start exploring, experimenting, and enhancing your videos with the incredible range of royalty-free media available. Remember, the goal is to use these resources to tell your story, your way. The only limit is your creativity.

And when you do find success with integrating royalty-free media into your content strategy, consider sharing the knowledge. Building a community that supports and informs can only make the content creator space richer. Who knows? Your insights might spark inspiration in another creator's journey.

With this guide to finding and using royalty-free media, you're now equipped to take your content to new heights. It's a journey of continuous learning and creativity, but with these tools at your disposal, the path is clearer. Embrace the challenge, keep innovating, and most importantly, have fun creating.

Editing Tools and Software Recommendations

Jumping right into the arsenal that'll turn your raw footage into engaging content, we've got to talk about the editing tools and software that can make or break your YouTube channel. The right software doesn't just polish your videos; it makes the process a breeze, keeping that creative juice flowing without interruption.

First off, let's acknowledge that budget plays a big role here. But, guess what? You don't need to break the bank to get professional results. There are free and affordable editing software options that pack a powerful punch. DaVinci Resolve is a prime example. It's robust, with color correction and audio post-production features that could rival expensive counterparts. Perfect for creators ready to step up their game without emptying their wallets.

On the flip side, if you're able to invest a bit more, Adobe Premiere Pro is a treasure trove of features. It integrates seamlessly with other Adobe apps, making it a solid choice for a streamlined workflow. Its versatility is unmatched, whether you're slicing together quick vlogs or crafting cinematic masterpieces.

Not to overlook the beginners, software like iMovie for Mac users or HitFilm Express offers user-friendly interfaces with surprisingly comprehensive editing tools. They're fantastic starting points that encourage experimentation without the overwhelm.

For those who are always on the move, don't fret. Mobile editing apps like KineMaster or Adobe Premiere Rush bring considerable power to your fingertips, enabling you to edit on your phone or tablet anywhere, anytime. These apps demonstrate that you don't need a fancy setup to start creating; just start with what you have.

Now, speaking of features, understanding your needs is crucial. Do you require advanced color grading capabilities, or are you mostly cutting clips and adding transitions? Not every editor needs a software equipped with 3D modeling capabilities, but if your channel thrives on animated content, Blender might just be your best friend.

Efficiency is key. Look for software that offers presets and templates. These can drastically reduce your editing time, allowing you to maintain a consistent look across your videos with minimal effort. It's all about working smarter, not harder.

Collaboration features are a must for teams. Software like Frame.io offers cloud-based collaboration for creators who need to share projects and feedback without being in the same room. It's a game-changer for ensuring everyone is on the same page, regardless of where they are in the world.

Don't get too caught up on the "best" software out there. The best is what works for you—your budget, your skill level, and your content needs. Experiment with different tools; many offer free trials that give you a taste of what they can do without committing financially.

Audio editing deserves a shoutout too. Audacity and Adobe Audition are excellent for polishing your sound, removing background noise, and ensuring your audio is as crisp as your visuals. Remember, poor audio quality can be a major turn-off for viewers, even more so than video quality.

Once you've chosen your tools, invest time in learning them. Plenty of tutorials are available online that can transform you from a novice to a pro in no time. The investment in your education is just as important as the investment in the software itself.

Integration is something many overlook. Your editing software should play nice with other tools you use, like your camera and any graphics software. This compatibility will streamline your process, saving you time and frustration in the long run.

Lastly, think about the future. Choose software that can grow with you. Starting simple is fine, but consider whether your chosen tool will meet your needs as your channel expands, and you start pushing the boundaries of your creativity.

In conclusion, your creative vision deserves the right set of tools to bring it to life. With the multitude of software options out there, there's something for every type of creator. It's about finding that sweet spot between functionality, budget, and ease of use. Let your editing software be the unsung hero of your faceless YouTube channel, working behind the scenes to turn your ideas into engaging, visually appealing content that captivates your audience. Keep experimenting, keep learning, and most importantly, keep creating.

Building Efficient Production Workflows

Let's get one thing straight – building an efficient production workflow is your golden ticket to not just surviving but thriving in the bustling world of faceless YouTube channels. Imagine this as setting up a well-oiled machine that generates engaging content while you focus on scaling and exploring new opportunities. Sounds like a dream, right? Well, it's absolutely achievable.

First off, you need to map out your entire production process from idea generation to publishing. This might seem like a daunting task, but breaking it down into manageable steps can simplify things considerably. Think of it as building a LEGO set; each piece has its place and purpose. This visual mapping will help you identify any bottlenecks or inefficiencies that can be optimized.

One of the key components of an efficient workflow is batching. Instead of hopping from task to task, dedicate blocks of time to similar tasks. For instance, spend a day brainstorming and outlining several video ideas. Next, block out a time for scripting them all in one go. This method not only saves time but also helps maintain a consistent quality and tone across your content.

Organization plays a huge role in efficiency. Utilize tools like Trello, Asana, or even a simple spreadsheet to keep track of your production schedule. This ensures that you're always ahead of your content calendar, leaving no room for last-minute rushes that compromise quality.

Invest in the right tools and software that complement your workflow. While free tools can be great when you're starting out, there comes a point when investing in professional software pays off in the long run. This could mean faster editing times, higher-quality outputs, or more advanced features that allow your creativity to flourish.

Another workflow game-changer is creating templates where possible. Whether it's video thumbnails, intros, outros, or even certain repetitive segments in your videos, templates can drastically reduce your production time. It moreover ensures a consistent look and feel across your channel, which is key to brand recognition.

Outsourcing can also be a valuable tool in your arsenal. Certain tasks, like editing or scriptwriting, can be outsourced to professionals, freeing you up to focus on other aspects of your channel. It's important to weigh the costs versus the benefits, but many successful YouTubers rely on a team to keep their content machine running smoothly.

Don't forget to regularly review and refine your workflow. What worked when you were just starting out may not be as efficient now that you're scaling. Always be on the lookout for new tools, techniques, and strategies that can help improve your production process.

Feedback is a goldmine for efficiency. Regularly check in with your team, if you have one, or seek advice from fellow creators. Sometimes, a fresh pair of eyes can spot a hiccup in your workflow that you might have overlooked.

Embrace automation wherever possible. Various aspects of content creation and channel management can be automated with the right tools. From scheduling uploads to organizing your content calendar, automation tools can save you a ton of time and effort.

Mental and physical health is another aspect that's critical yet often overlooked in the hustle culture. Ensure that your workflow includes breaks and allows for a healthy work-life balance. Burnout is real and can set you and your channel back significantly if not managed properly.

Collaboration can also streamline your workflow. Teaming up with other creators for certain projects not only shares the workload but brings in fresh ideas and perspectives. Plus, it's a great way to cross-promote content and grow your audience.

Setting realistic deadlines is crucial. It's better to plan for a sustainable pace of content release that ensures quality rather than rushing to meet unrealistic expectations. This might require some experimentation in the beginning to find what rhythm works best for your channel.

Lastly, remember why you started. Keep your passion alive by regularly experimenting with new ideas and pushing your creative boundaries. An efficient workflow shouldn't mean a rigid, monotonous production line. It should give you the freedom to innovate and explore new frontiers in content creation.

Building an efficient production workflow for your faceless YouTube channel is a dynamic, ongoing process. It requires patience, experimentation, and a continuous desire to improve. With the right approach, tools, and mindset, you can create a workflow that not only maximizes productivity but also fuels your creative passion. And that, my friend, is the essence of a truly successful faceless YouTube channel.

Chapter 5

Optimizing Videos for SEO

Diving right into the heart of making your faceless YouTube channel a hit, optimizing your videos for SEO is like fine-tuning your arrow's aim to hit that bullseye—every single time. Think of each video you release as a mini-campaign, one that could potentially skyrocket your visibility on YouTube's vast platform. It's not just about throwing content out there and hoping it sticks. It's about strategic moves; starting with deep-dive keyword research to understand exactly what your audience is searching for. This isn't about quick fixes; it's about crafting video titles, descriptions, and tags that are not only click-worthy but also rank-worthy.

And let's not forget the visuals—your thumbnails need to shout "click me" in an ocean of endless content. It's your first impression, your handshake, your smile to potential viewers, making them choose you over countless others. This chapter is your blueprint to master these elements, to weave SEO into your video's DNA. From tags that weave a wider net for your content to hashtags that categorize your content more effectively, you're about to become an SEO wizard. Remember, SEO isn't just about appeasing algorithms; it's about connecting your content with people who are searching for it, making your channel a beacon for your target audience. Let's turn that invisibility cloak off and illuminate your channel like a lighthouse in the vast sea of content.

Keyword Research for YouTube

Let's dive into one of the most critical aspects of optimizing videos for SEO on YouTube: keyword research. This is where the magic starts, and honestly, it's a game-changer when done right. Imagine being able to peek into the viewers' minds, understanding exactly what they're searching for. That's what effective keyword research allows you to do.

First things first, keyword research isn't just about finding high-volume search terms. It's about finding the right terms that your target audience is using. It means thinking like your viewer. Ask yourself, what would someone type into YouTube's search bar if they were looking for a video like mine? This perspective is your golden ticket. Remember, it's not just about getting any viewers; it's about getting the right viewers.

Now, where do you start? YouTube's own search bar is a gold mine. Begin typing in a phrase related to your niche, and observe the suggestions that appear. These suggestions are not random; they're what real people are actively searching for. Jot these down, because they're your first clues into the minds of your audience.

But let's not stop there. Use tools designed for this very purpose. Google Trends, for example, is fantastic for comparing keyword popularity over time. Then there's TubeBuddy and VidIQ, both offer specific features geared towards finding keywords that can help your videos gain visibility. These tools can show you search volumes, competition, and even suggest related keywords you might not have considered.

Competition is something you'll need to pay close attention to. It's great to find a keyword with high search volume, but if the competition is fierce, your video might struggle to be seen. Look for those sweet spots - keywords with decent search volumes but lower competition. These are your gateways to visibility.

Don't forget, it's not just about the main keyword. Long-tail keywords, which are longer and more specific phrases, can be incredibly valuable. They might have lower search volumes, but they also tend to have less competition and a more targeted audience. Incorporating these into your content strategy can lead to higher engagement rates and more dedicated viewers.

Integration of keywords into your video content is equally important. Once you've identified your target keywords, they should naturally flow in your video's title, description, and even your spoken content. YouTube's algorithms are smart, and they can pick up on these cues to understand what your video is about and who might want to see it.

But beware of the trap of keyword stuffing. This practice, where keywords are overused or added unnaturally, can hurt your video's performance. Use them smartly and sparingly, ensuring your content remains engaging and authentic.

Testing and refinement should become your routine practices. The world of YouTube is always evolving, and so are search behaviors. Keep an eye on your video performance metrics and be ready to adjust your keyword strategy as needed. What works today might not work tomorrow, and staying adaptable is key.

Collaboration can also play a role in your keyword research process. Engaging with fellow creators, especially those in your niche, can offer new insights and perspectives on effective keywords. Sometimes, a fresh set of eyes can spot opportunities you might have missed.

Educating yourself regularly is part of the game. The landscape of SEO and keywords changes often, so staying informed through online resources, courses, or webinars will keep your strategies sharp and effective.

Remember, keyword research is an ongoing journey. It's not just a one-off task to tick off your list. The more you do it, the more intuitive it becomes. You'll start to see patterns, understand nuances in viewer behavior, and discover new opportunities to connect with your audience.

Your ultimate goal is to make your content as discoverable as possible, and mastering keyword research is a significant step in that direction. It enhances your video's ability to reach the right viewers, at the right time, with the right content. It's about being visible in that vast ocean of content and standing out as a beacon for your target audience.

And finally, let's keep this in perspective. Keyword research is crucial, but it's just one piece of the SEO puzzle. Your content needs to deliver value once viewers click through. Balancing SEO tactics with high-quality, engaging content is what will ultimately build your channel's success. You've got this. The path to mastering your faceless YouTube channel and generating that coveted passive income starts with taking that first step. Dive deep into keyword research and let it guide your content to the forefront of your target audience's search results.

As you continue through this journey, remember the power you wield with the right keywords. They are not just words; they're the keys to unlocking the vast potential of your faceless YouTube channel. Harness this power, and you're on your way to not just reaching, but exceeding your goals.

Writing Click-Worthy Titles and Descriptions

Now, let's dive deep into the art of creating titles and descriptions that not just catch the eye but make the viewer click without a second thought. It's all about striking a balance. You want to be catchy, but not clickbaity; informative, but not dull. Let's start with titles, the gateway to your video content. They're like the cover of a book, and in the digital age, people often do judge a book by its cover—or in this case, a video by its title.

Your title needs to pack a punch. It should be a beacon that guides your target audience through the vast ocean of content on YouTube. It's not just about throwing in relevant keywords; it's about making those keywords work for you in a way that piques interest. Think about what makes your video unique. Have you debunked a common myth? Solved a problem in a novel way? Your title should reflect that. Imagine a title like "5 Unheard Ways to Boost Your Productivity." It's specific, offers value, and has a hint of mystery to it.

But let's not forget descriptions. They're your space to expand upon the teaser that your title provides. Here, you get to tell a story. Begin with a hook—a compelling first line that continues the intrigue your title has started. Then, outline what viewers can expect without giving it all away. Think of it as setting the table for a feast of content that's too tempting to pass up.

Keywords play a huge part here, too. But it's not about stuffing them where they don't naturally fit. It's about seamless integration into your descriptions, making them search-friendly yet still engaging to read. Always include a call-to-action, as well. This could be asking your viewers to subscribe, share your video, or check out other related content on your channel. Engagement doesn't just happen. You have to encourage it.

What's also crucial is making use of metadata smartly. YouTube's algorithm loves videos that make it easy to understand what they're about. That means your titles, descriptions, and even tags need to work in harmony. Think of these elements as the SEO trifecta that, when used correctly, can significantly boost your video's visibility and, ultimately, its success.

Let's talk specifics. When crafting your titles and descriptions, focus on clarity and conciseness. Viewers or potential viewers should grasp what your video is about in a heartbeat. This doesn't mean you can't be creative or playful. In fact, creativity sets you apart. But it's essential to ensure your creativity serves to enlighten, not confuse.

Another tip is to keep an eye on what's trending. Use tools available to you to understand current trends within your niche. Jumping on a trend could be a fantastic way to get your video seen by a wider audience. However, ensure that the trend aligns with your channel's content and values. You want to attract viewers who will stick around for more.

Use numbers and lists in your titles when appropriate. "Top 10..." or "5 Steps to..." are examples of titles that practically have viewers clicking before they've even finished reading. There's something about numbers that promise a structured, easy-to-digest video. But again, relevance is key. Don't throw in a number if your video doesn't genuinely deliver on that promise.

Create a sense of urgency. Titles that suggest the viewer will miss out if they don't watch your video can be incredibly effective. Phrases like "Don't Miss," "Before You Buy," or "Limited Time" can make your video irresistible. But, as always, authenticity is critical. False urgency can backfire and erode trust in your brand.

Testing different titles and descriptions is another strategy that's often overlooked. Don't be afraid to change things up if you notice certain videos aren't performing as well as others. A/B testing can provide valuable insights into what resonates with your audience. Remember, YouTube provides analytics for a reason. Use them to guide your optimization strategies.

Descriptions also offer a valuable space to include links to your social media profiles, merchandise, or patreon. This doesn't just serve as a way to grow your follower count or increase your revenue streams; it makes it easier for viewers to connect with you on different platforms, deepening their engagement with your brand.

Lastly, don't overlook the power of storytelling. Even your SEO efforts should tell a story. From the title to the description to the video content itself, you're taking viewers on a journey. Make it a journey worth embarking on. Capture their curiosity, and more importantly, keep it.

Keep refining your skills. Writing click-worthy titles and descriptions is as much an art as it is a science. The digital landscape is always changing, and what works today may not work tomorrow. Stay curious, keep learning, and always be ready to adapt. The success of your faceless YouTube channel depends on it.

Remember, each video is an opportunity to reach new heights. Don't see it as just another upload. See it as a chance to capture attention, entertain, inform, and inspire. With the right titles and descriptions, your videos won't just be seen; they'll be remembered. That's the power of effective SEO optimization. It's not just about playing the algorithm game; it's about making genuine connections through captivating storytelling. That's your ticket to building a successful, sustainable faceless YouTube channel that thrives on passive income.

Crafting Eye-Catching Thumbnails

Let's dive into one of the most critical yet often underrated aspects of optimizing videos for SEO: crafting eye-catching thumbnails. It might seem like just a small part of your video, but think of your thumbnail as the front door to your content. It's the first thing viewers lay their eyes on and can make or break their decision to click on your video. So, let's get it right and make sure that door is as inviting as possible.

First off, think of your thumbnail as a visual promise to your potential viewers. It needs to capture the essence of your video in a single, compelling image. This means clarity is key. You want to create an image that's easily understood at a glance, but still intriguing enough to make viewers want to find out more. A common mistake is overcrowding the thumbnail with too much detail, which can lead to confusion.

Color plays a massive role in catching viewer's eyes. Use bold, contrasting colors to make your thumbnail stand out in the sea of videos. However, make sure these colors align with your brand or the mood of the video content. This consistency helps in building a visual identity for your channel, making your content easily recognizable amongst your audience.

The use of text in your thumbnails should be approached with a minimalist mindset. Ideally, if text is necessary, it should complement the image and not cover or detract from it. Choose font sizes and styles that are legible even on smaller screens, and keep the wording succinct and punchy. The text is there to add context or create intrigue, not to explain the entire video.

Emotion drives action. If your video content allows, feature facial expressions in your thumbnails. Viewers are naturally drawn to human faces, especially those that convey strong emotions, whether it's joy, surprise, or curiosity. An expressive face can be a powerful way to connect with potential viewers and increase the likelihood of them clicking on your video.

It's essential to maintain a high resolution and quality in your thumbnails. Remember, your thumbnail represents the quality of your video. A pixelated or blurry thumbnail might give off the impression that your video is of low quality, deterring viewers. Aim for sharp, clear images that look professional.

Personalizing thumbnails can also make a significant difference. If your faceless channel revolves around certain themes or characters, incorporate those into your thumbnails. Custom illustrations, recognizable motifs, or consistent color schemes can go a long way in making your thumbnails—and your channel—stand out.

Moreover, testing and iterating your thumbnails is a key step that shouldn't be overlooked. Platforms like YouTube offer analytics that allow you to see how well your thumbnails are performing in terms of click-through rate. Experiment with different designs, colors, and text to see what resonates best with your target audience. This data-driven approach can help you refine your thumbnail strategy over time.

Let's talk about branding. While keeping thumbnails eye-catching, incorporating a subtle brand element, be it a logo, a specific border style, or a recurring character, helps in fostering brand recognition. This consistency aids viewers in immediately recognizing your content in their recommendations or search results.

Remember, the goal of your thumbnail is not to deceive. It's easy to fall into the trap of creating 'clickbait' thumbnails that don't accurately represent the video content. This can hurt your channel in the long run, as viewers will quickly lose trust in your content. Ensure your thumbnails are honest representations of your videos, teasing the content without giving it all away.

Consider the platform norms when designing thumbnails. YouTube, for instance, has its set of best practices for thumbnails. These include avoiding the use of excessive text, not using images that might be misleading or clickbaity, and considering how your thumbnail will look on both desktop and mobile devices.

Don't forget about accessibility. While designing your thumbnails, consider those in your audience who might have visual impairments. Use high contrast color schemes and clear, readable fonts to ensure your thumbnails are accessible to everyone.

Incorporating trends into your thumbnails can also capture viewer interest. However, it's important to balance trendiness with timelessness. You want your thumbnails to feel current but not quickly become dated. Observing what's popular in your niche and finding creative ways to integrate those elements can make your videos more appealing.

Lastly, be patient. Developing the skill to create effective thumbnails takes time. Each video is a new opportunity to learn and improve.

Take inspiration from successful channels in your niche, but always aim to infuse your unique style and creativity.

In conclusion, crafting eye-catching thumbnails is an art as much as it is a science. It's about combining aesthetics with data to create a visual hook that draws viewers in. With practice, patience, and persistence, you'll find the formula that works best for your faceless YouTube channel, elevating your SEO game and driving more views and engagement your way. Remember, your thumbnail is your first impression—make it count.

Best Practices for Tags and Hashtags

So, you've got your video ready to go, and you're about to hit that upload button. Wait a sec! Have you thought about your tags and hashtags? These little guys are mighty when it comes to YouTube SEO. They're like the secret sauce that gets your videos discovered. So, how do you use them effectively? Let's dive in.

First off, tags. Think of tags as keywords for your video. They help YouTube understand the content and context of your video. This is crucial because YouTube's algorithm uses this info to decide when and where to show your video. Start with your main keyword, then add variations of this keyword and other related terms. Keep it relevant, though. Throwing in random popular tags won't do you any favors and might even hurt your video's visibility.

Now, you might be wondering, "How many tags should I use?" While YouTube allows up to 500 characters in the tags section, quality over quantity is the mantra here. Aim for 15 to 20 well-chosen tags that accurately describe your video's content, context, and your intended audience. This balance ensures you're covering enough ground without spamming irrelevant tags.

On to hashtags. These are a newer addition to the YouTube game but they're gaining traction fast. Hashtags in your video description can increase your video's reach by making it discoverable in hashtag searches. Think Twitter, but on YouTube. The catch? You can include as many as you want, but only the first three hashtags you use will show up above your video title.

Choosing the right hashtags starts with understanding your content and your audience. Include hashtags that are specific to the video's topic, but also consider broader hashtags that relate to your video's overarching theme. This mix can help you attract both niche viewers and those just browsing.

Now, a word of caution. Don't go overboard. YouTube might penalize your video for using irrelevant or misleading tags and hashtags. Stick to what accurately represents your video. This integrity not only respects your audience's time but also builds trust with YouTube's algorithms.

Let's talk strategy. For tags, start with a mix of broad and specific terms. Broad terms get you on the map, while specific terms connect you with viewers looking for exactly what you've got. For example, if your video is about making perfect latte art, your tags might include "coffee," "latte art," and "how to make latte art."

For hashtags, think trends and community. Jumping on trending hashtags can give your video a temporary boost in views. But, connecting with a community (like #SmallYouTubers) can help establish your channel in a supportive network. Balancing trending and community hashtags can propel your video into new audiences.

Experimentation is your best friend here. YouTube's analytics allow you to see how viewers are discovering your videos. Play around with different tags and hashtags, check the analytics, and refine your strategy. What works for one video might not work for another, and what works today might need tweaking tomorrow. Stay curious and adaptable.

Another pro tip is to use YouTube's auto-suggest feature. Start typing in your tag or hashtag in the search bar and see what YouTube suggests. This can give you insight into popular search terms and phrases that you might not have considered.

Let's not forget about branded hashtags. If you're building a brand or a series, create a unique hashtag for your viewers to follow and use. This not only cultivates a community but also helps in tracking your brand's reach on YouTube.

Remember, tags and hashtags are not a set-it-and-forget-it deal. Revisit your older videos periodically and update tags and hashtags as trends change and new keywords emerge. This ongoing optimization keeps your content fresh and findable.

Incorporating these best practices for tags and hashtags into your YouTube strategy takes a bit of effort upfront, but it's an investment in your channel's growth. With the right tags and hashtags, your videos can reach farther and connect with viewers who are eager for exactly what you offer. You've got the content; now, let's make sure it gets the spotlight it deserves.

And there you have it, the lowdown on leveraging tags and hashtags to turbocharge your video's visibility on YouTube. Armed with these strategies, you're not just throwing content into the void; you're strategically placing it where viewers are most likely to stumble upon it. Get tagging, get hashtagging, and watch your faceless YouTube channel thrive.

Remember, every detail counts in the grand scheme of YouTube success. Tags and hashtags might seem small, but they're part of the bigger puzzle of SEO that can make or break your visibility. Use them wisely, keep experimenting, and never stop optimizing. Your next viral video might just be one well-chosen hashtag away.

Chapter 6

Uploading and Publishing Videos

Now that you've crafted your masterpiece, it's time to share it with the world, and trust me, there's an art to uploading and publishing your videos that can really make a difference in how they perform. Think of it as setting the stage for your video to shine. First off, the timing of your upload isn't just a detail—it's crucial. You want your video to hit the ground running the moment your audience is most active. That's where scheduling comes into play, allowing your content to land in viewers' laps exactly when they're most likely to watch it. But it doesn't stop there; utilizing end screens and cards can guide your viewers through your channel like a well-thought-out tour, increasing their viewing time and engagement with your content.

Subtitles and closed captions might seem like a chore but consider this: not only do they make your videos accessible to a wider audience, including those who are hearing impaired, but they also cater to viewers who prefer watching videos without sound, which is a larger segment than you might think. Also, let's not forget about the global audience who might rely on translations of your captions to enjoy your content. Every aspect of the upload and publication process, from the technical to the strategic, is an opportunity to extend your reach and impact. As you master this process, you'll find it becomes a powerful part of your content strategy, turning uploads from mere technicalities into strategic moves that drive your channel's success.

The Perfect Upload Routine

Let's talk about something that could very well be the game-changer in your faceless YouTube channel journey: the perfect upload routine. It's like having a secret recipe that, when followed, can significantly increase your channel's chance of success. Keep in mind, this isn't about cutting corners or a one-size-fits-all solution; it's about efficiency, consistency, and engaging your audience in the absolute best way possible.

First up, consistency is key. I can't stress enough how crucial this is. Your subscribers and potential viewers thrive on predictability; they love knowing when to expect new content from you. This doesn't mean you have to upload daily – that's unrealistic for most – but setting a schedule, whether it's once a week or bi-weekly, and sticking to it is vital. This routine helps keep your channel in the viewers' minds and algorithms' favor.

Before you hit that publish button, though, let's dial it back to the crucial step of optimizing your video during the upload. We're talking titles, descriptions, tags, and thumbnails. These elements are your video's handshake with the world, the first impression, and you want it to be a good one. Your title should be clear but catchy, incorporating keywords, while your description can go more in-depth, offering context and more keyword opportunities. Tags help categorize your video, making it more discoverable, and an eye-catching thumbnail? That's the visual hook for clicks.

Speaking of hooks, don't underestimate the power of a strong opening in your video. The first few seconds are critical in retaining viewers' attention. Make sure your intro delivers on what the title and thumbnail promise; this alignment keeps trust with your audience.

Once your video is optimized and ready to go, think about timing. YouTube analytics can be a goldmine for determining when most of your audience is online. Scheduling your uploads to go live during these peak times can increase initial views, which is crucial for signaling to YouTube that your video is worth promoting.

But what happens after the upload? Promotion shouldn't end there. Share your video across your social media platforms, embed it in blogs or websites if relevant, and even consider sending it out via email to your list if you have one. This multi-platform approach maximizes your video's initial exposure, crucial for gathering momentum.

Engagement doesn't end with posting elsewhere; it's also about being present on your own video. Reply to comments, pin top comments, and interact with your community. This activity not only bolsters community building but it's also looked upon favorably by YouTube's algorithms.

Let's also hash out the importance of analytics post-upload. Your job isn't done when the video is live; it's just begun. Dive into your YouTube analytics to understand how your video is performing. Watch time, click-through rate, and retention rate are all critical metrics. Leverage this data for future content planning, tweaking your strategy based on what's resonating with your viewers.

Now, for a hot take: don't be afraid to update your video's metadata (title, tags, description) post-publish if it's not performing as expected. YouTube's algorithms are always on the lookout for relevant, engaging content, and sometimes a slight tweak can give your video a second wind.

Remember, the perfect upload routine is not just about the act of uploading but everything that surrounds it – from the strategic timing to ongoing engagement and analytics review. It's a holistic approach designed to give your content the best possible chance to shine on a platform that's crowded yet filled with opportunities.

Adopting a routine might seem daunting at first, but it's like any good habit – give it time, and it'll become second nature. Plus, the more you practice, the more intuitive these steps will become, freeing up more of your energy for creativity and innovation in your content.

Motivation is a mandatory passenger on this journey. There will be days when the last thing you want to do is think about keywords or analyze viewer demographics. But remind yourself of the big picture: each step in this routine is a brick in the foundation of your channel's growth and your road to passive income. Keep your eyes on the prize, and remember why you started.

Lastly, let's embrace patience and resilience. Your perfect upload routine might undergo several iterations before you find what truly works for you and your channel. That's okay. The YouTube landscape is incredibly dynamic, with viewer behaviors and platform algorithms constantly evolving. Staying adaptable, learning from each upload, and pushing forward with determination is the secret sauce for long-term success.

So, take these insights and craft your perfect upload routine. It's one of the many tools in your arsenal as a creator, and when wielded correctly, it's incredibly powerful. Treat it with the importance it deserves, and you'll be setting yourself up for remarkable achievements on your faceless YouTube channel. Let the uploading begin!

Scheduling Videos for Maximum Impact

Let's dive into one of the most crucial strategies in your content journey—scheduling your videos for maximum impact. Timing isn't just about when; it's about striking when the iron is hot to ensure your content gets in front of as many eyes as possible. This isn't a guessing game. It's an art and science, peppered with a dash of strategy to boost your videos' performance significantly.

Understanding your audience's viewing habits is paramount. Think about who they are, where they're from, and when they're most likely to scroll for new content. Different audiences have different peak times. Are your viewers early birds or night owls? Weekend warriors or weekday warriors? These nuances matter because timing your uploads to match your audience's schedule increases your chances of catching them right when they're online.

Analyzing your channel's analytics is your treasure map. YouTube provides a wealth of data showing when your viewers are online. This isn't just handy; it's your secret weapon. By tailoring your upload schedule to these insights, you're not shooting in the dark. You're strategically placing your content where it can't be missed.

Consistency is your best friend here. It's not just about the day or time; it's about the regularity. Viewers love predictability. They want to know when they can expect new content from you. Establishing a consistent upload schedule trains your audience to anticipate your videos, creating a habit loop that keeps them coming back for more.

But here's the key—don't let the quest for perfect timing paralyze you. The best schedule is one you can stick to. If life happens and you need to adjust, that's fine. Your audience will understand, especially if you communicate with them. The importance of consistency cannot be overstated, but flexibility is equally important.

Holiday seasons and special events present unique opportunities. Tailoring content around these times can give your videos an added boost. Think about it—during holidays, people are more likely to have free time and be in a festive mood, making them more receptive to certain types of content. Capitalizing on this can make a huge difference in your views and engagement.

But it's not just about the when; it's also about the how. When scheduling your uploads, consider the cascade effect. Your latest video can drive viewers to your older content, too. Intelligently linking videos through end screens and playlists as part of your scheduling strategy can amplify this effect, maximizing viewership across your channel.

Also, think beyond just YouTube. Your video promotion strategy on social media platforms can benefit from smart scheduling, too. Share teasers, behind-the-scenes looks, or snippets on your other channels to create buzz right before your main video goes live. Aligning these posts with your upload schedule keeps your content top of mind for your audience.

Be mindful, though, of YouTube's algorithm. It favors engagement and retention, so while scheduling is crucial, the quality of your content holds the final card. Your goal is to maximize visibility, but never compromise the integrity and value of your videos for the sake of timing. Engaging, high-quality content will always come out on top.

Experimentation is key. Even with all the data in the world, there's always room for testing. Try uploading at different times and days to see what works best for your channel. Keep an eye on the performance metrics and be ready to pivot. This isn't a set-it-and-forget-it deal. It's an ongoing process of refinement.

Let's not forget about time zones. If your audience is global, finding a sweet spot can be tricky. In such cases, aim for a time that hits the majority of your audience when they're likely to be online. You might not please everyone, but you can maximize your reach within your largest viewer segments.

Advance scheduling features are a godsend. YouTube's ability to schedule videos in advance is a feature you should be leveraging. It allows you to upload and set your videos to go live at your chosen time, giving you the freedom to work ahead of schedule. This is particularly handy for maintaining consistency, even when you're not physically available to hit 'publish.'

Lastly, remember that community feedback is invaluable. Engage with your audience and ask them directly about their preferred watching times. Including them in the process not only gives you direct insights but also strengthens the bond with your viewers. It shows them their opinions matter, fostering a stronger community around your channel.

The journey to finding the perfect scheduling sweet spot for your videos is ongoing. Trends change, algorithms update, and audience behaviors shift. Staying adaptable, informed, and attentive to these changes will help you refine your scheduling strategy for maximum impact. But the most important piece of advice? Start now. The best time to refine your upload strategy was yesterday—the second-best time is today.

In conclusion, while mastering the art of scheduling might seem daunting at first, it's a powerful tool in your YouTube arsenal. With a strategic approach, informed by insights and tailored to your audience's habits, you can significantly boost your video's performance. Remember, success on YouTube isn't just about creating great content—it's also about making sure it gets seen by the right people at the right time.

Using End Screens and Cards Effectively

Let's dive into a game-changer in your YouTube journey—mastering the art of using end screens and cards. These tools, albeit small in the grand scheme of your video, pack a massive punch in boosting your channel's viewership and engagement. When you're looking to create a seamless viewer experience and guide your audience to more of your content, these features become indispensable.

End screens are those last few seconds of your video where you can showcase other video recommendations, prompt viewers to subscribe, or direct them to external websites. Think of them as your virtual "See You Later" sign, guiding viewers where you want them to go next. It's about keeping the engagement ball rolling even as one video ends.

On the other hand, cards are the subtle nudges during a video that can direct viewers to related content, polls, external links, and more. They're like the gentle tap on the shoulder in a crowded room, saying, "Hey, check this out." These cards, when used smartly, can significantly increase your channel's watch time and viewer interaction.

The power of an effectively placed end screen cannot be overstated. As your video wraps up, and you deliver your closing remarks, that's your golden moment. Use it wisely by suggesting two to four selections of your content that are not only relevant but also interesting to the viewer based on the video they just watched. Matching the recommendation to the viewer's interests increases the chance they'll click and keep watching.

Now, let's talk customization. YouTube's platform allows you to tailor your end screens in ways that resonate best with your audience. Whether it's the design layout, the choice of videos to promote, or the call-to-action for subscriptions, you have the freedom to experiment. Remember, the goal is to make it as easy as possible for viewers to take the next step in their viewing journey with you.

Cards, sprinkled thoughtfully throughout your video, are your engagement enhancers. Use them to ask questions, direct viewers to other videos, or even get them to participate in a poll. This not only increases interaction but also gives you valuable insights into your audience's preferences and thoughts.

But remember, timing is key with cards. You want to insert them at moments when they'll be most effective and least disruptive.

Dropping in a card just as you're making a critical point might distract your viewers, so look for natural pauses or transitional moments in your content to slot these in.

Another strategic use of end screens and cards is to direct traffic to external sites. If you're running an e-commerce site or a blog in addition to your YouTube channel, these features can be a goldmine for driving traffic. Use them to promote merchandise, upcoming events, or more detailed information related to your video's content.

A tip for success is to keep a close eye on your analytics. YouTube provides detailed data on how your end screens and cards are performing. Are your viewers clicking through? At what point do they tend to drop off? Use this data to tweak your approach, test different strategies, and find what resonates best with your audience.

Incorporating calls-to-action within your video script is also crucial. Let your viewers know what to expect at the end of the video or when a card pops up. A simple, "Don't forget to check out my other videos popping up right now," can work wonders in guiding viewers to take action.

Flexibility and experimentation are your best friends here. Not every strategy will work for every type of content or audience. You might find that end screens work better for certain videos, while cards generate more engagement in others. Keep testing different designs, layouts, and calls to action to see what brings the best results.

Engage with your community through these features. Use cards to link to community posts or ask for feedback through polls. This not only boosts your engagement metrics but also builds a stronger connection with your audience. They'll appreciate being involved in your content creation process.

Lastly, consistency is key. While it's important to experiment, once you find something that works, stick with it. Consistent use of end screens and cards not only improves overall viewer experience but also reinforces your branding. Over time, your audience will come to expect and look forward to your recommendations and prompts.

To wrap it up, leveraging end screens and cards effectively can significantly enhance your viewer's experience and engagement on your channel. It's about making smart, strategic decisions that guide your audience seamlessly through your content ecosystem. Keep experimenting, analyzing, and engaging with your viewers through these features, and watch as your faceless YouTube channel grows and thrives. Remember, every little detail counts in the grand chess game of YouTube success.

Embrace these tools, and let them work wonders for your channel. With a bit of creativity and strategic thinking, end screens and cards can become powerful allies in your journey to creating a successful, income-generating faceless YouTube channel. Go out there, create compelling content, and use every tool at your disposal to keep your viewers engaged and coming back for more.

Subtitles, Closed Captions, and Transcriptions

Jumping into the world of YouTube with a faceless channel means you're about to embark on a journey that not only involves creating engaging content but also ensuring it reaches as wide an audience as possible. An often overlooked yet critical aspect of making your videos more accessible and SEO-friendly is the use of subtitles, closed captions, and transcriptions. Let's dive deeper into why these elements are your silent growth partners in the bustling YouTube universe.

First off, subtitles and closed captions might seem interchangeable, but they serve slightly different purposes. Subtitles primarily exist to translate dialogue for viewers who understand the video's language but might not be able to hear the audio. On the other hand, closed captions are designed for viewers who are deaf or hard of hearing, providing not only dialogue but also non-speech elements like sound effects or speaker identification. Incorporating these not only boosts accessibility but also keeps your content in line with global inclusivity standards.

Transcriptions take this a step further by converting your entire video's audio into text form, serving a dual purpose. For one, it makes your content consumable even in text format, reaching individuals who prefer reading over watching. Secondly, and more importantly from a growth perspective, it can significantly enhance your SEO efforts. How? By providing search engines with a rich source of keywords directly related to your video content, making it more likely for your videos to pop up in search results.

Now, you might be thinking, "Sounds good, but isn't adding subtitles and captions a ton of work?" It's a valid concern, but thankfully, technology has our back. YouTube's automatic captioning feature offers a starting point, generating captions for your videos with the click of a button. However, it's not perfect and often needs a human touch to correct inaccuracies. This is where you come in, investing a bit of time to refine these automated captions, thus making your videos far more accessible and enjoyable for all viewers.

But let's not stop there. Creating custom subtitles and captions in various languages can exponentially increase your channel's reach, breaking language barriers and tapping into non-English speaking audiences. Imagine your content resonating with viewers across continents, all because you took the extra step to include multilingual subtitles. Incredible, right?

In terms of transcriptions, you have a few options. Manual transcription is the most accurate but also the most time-consuming. Alternatively, automatic transcription tools can save time, though they may require some editing for accuracy. Whichever route you choose, posting video transcriptions on your channel's website or blog not only aids SEO but also enriches your site's content, giving viewers more ways to engage with your brand.

Let's not forget about the SEO bonanza we mentioned earlier. Keywords in your subtitles, captions, and transcriptions are like hidden treasure for search engines. Including targeted keywords naturally within these texts can help your videos rank higher, not just on YouTube, but also on Google searches. Think of each video as a multi-faceted gem, with its accessibility features multiplying its chances to shine in search results.

Moreover, viewer engagement can see a significant uptick thanks to subtitles and captions. People watching in noisy environments, or those who need a little extra help understanding the dialogue, will appreciate the text support. This inclusivity fosters a sense of belonging among your audience, encouraging them to stick around, engage, and even recommend your content to others.

Should you worry about the potential costs? While professional captioning services offer accuracy and quality, they can indeed be pricey. However, starting with YouTube's auto-generated captions and dedicating some time to manual corrections can be a budget-friendly compromise. As your channel grows, investing in professional services or multilingual subtitles could become a viable option, further expanding your audience.

Implementing these features is not just about compliance or ticking a box; it's about showing your audience that you value and respect their viewing preferences and needs. This can dramatically improve audience satisfaction and loyalty, turning casual viewers into dedicated fans.

It's also worth experimenting with different subtitle styles and formats to see what works best for your content and audience. YouTube offers customization options such as font, color, and size, allowing you to ensure that your subtitles enhance rather than distract from your videos.

Lastly, don't overlook the power of community contributions. Engaging your viewers in the captioning and translation process can foster a stronger community around your channel. YouTube's community contributions feature allows viewers to add captions, subtitles, and translations to videos, which you can then review and approve. This not only lightens your workload but also deepens viewer investment in your content.

In conclusion, subtitles, closed captions, and transcriptions might seem like small details in the grand scheme of creating and uploading videos. However, they're powerful tools that can significantly impact your channel's accessibility, viewer engagement, and search engine presence. By investing the time and effort into these elements, you're not just complying with best practices; you're taking a proactive step towards creating a more inclusive, discoverable, and engaging channel. That's a win for you, your audience, and the global community sharing in the content you create. Let these tools be your unsung heroes in the quest to conquer the YouTube landscape.

Remember, the journey to YouTube success is filled with small, cumulative steps. Subtitles, closed captions, and transcriptions are shining examples of these steps. Embrace them, and watch as they unlock new levels of growth and engagement for your faceless YouTube channel. Let's make your content not just seen, but heard, understood, and appreciated by as many people as possible. The world is waiting to hear what you have to say, so let's make sure everyone can understand it.

Chapter 7

Growing and Engaging Your Audience

Now that you've got the ball rolling with your faceless YouTube channel, it's time to shift gears and focus on what really turns the wheels in this game: your audience. Growing and engaging with your viewers isn't just about throwing content at them and hoping it sticks. Think of it as nurturing a garden. You've got to water it, give it plenty of sunshine, and yes, sometimes talk to the plants if you have to. Leveraging social media isn't just about cross-posting your latest video; it's about creating conversations and diving deep into communities where your content resonates. And remember, your audience is craving more than just videos; they want to be part of the story. Engaging with them through comments and polls not only gives them a voice but also invaluable insights for you to tailor your content and keep it fresh.

Breaking the fourth wall by collaborating with other creators can introduce your channel to audiences you never even dreamed of. Plus, it's a fantastic way to keep your content dynamic and exciting. But here's the kicker, none of this matters if you're not keeping an eye on what your audience thinks and feels. Diving into analytics might sound as appealing as watching paint dry, but trust me, understanding your audience's insights and feedback is like finding a treasure map that leads you to more views, more engagement, and ultimately, a thriving channel. So, let's get down to business and turn your channel into a bustling hub that viewers can't wait to return to.

Leveraging Social Media for Promotion

At this point in your journey, you've laid a solid foundation for your faceless YouTube channel. You've found your niche, crafted unique content, and honed in on your target audience. But, how do you catapult your channel from obscurity to visibility in an ocean of content? Enter the game-changer: social media promotion.

Think of social media not just as a casual hangout spot, but as an arsenal in your promotional toolkit. Each platform, be it Twitter, Instagram, Facebook, or Pinterest, serves a unique purpose and reaches different segments of your target audience. Leveraging these platforms effectively can amplify your reach, engage your audience, and drive traffic to your YouTube channel. Remember, the goal isn't to be everywhere; it's to be where your audience is.

Begin with a strategic approach. Identify which social media platforms your ideal viewers frequent the most. Are they scrolling through Instagram, tweeting up a storm, or pinning their favorite interests? Once you've zeroed in on the right platforms, create content tailored to each. An engaging Instagram story might not resonate the same way on Twitter, where quick, witty posts reign supreme.

Create a content calendar specific to your social media efforts. Timing is everything. Knowing when your audience is most active can make the difference between a post that sizzles and one that fizzles. Use scheduling tools to maintain a consistent presence without having to be online 24/7.

Engage, engage, engage. Social media is a two-way street. It's not just about broadcasting your message; it's about building relationships. Respond to comments, ask questions, and participate in relevant conversations. Show your audience you're not just a faceless entity but a vibrant, responsive creator who values their input and interaction.

Use hashtags intelligently. They're not just trendy; they're powerful tools for discoverability. Research and use hashtags that are relevant to your content and your audience. Joining in on trending topics can also increase your visibility, but ensure it aligns with your channel's theme and message.

Cross-promote your content. If you're active on multiple platforms, make sure your followers on one platform know about your presence on others. This doesn't mean spamming them with requests to follow you everywhere. Instead, offer them a reason to check out your other profiles, such as exclusive content or behind-the-scenes looks.

Collaborate with other creators and influencers. This can amplify your reach exponentially. Choose collaborators who share a similar target audience but aren't direct competitors. This not only exposes your channel to a broader audience but also builds camaraderie within the creator community.

Don't forget about the visual aspect. Social media is highly visual, so make sure the images and videos you share are eye-catching and high quality. This is especially true for platforms like Instagram and Pinterest, where visual content is king.

Incorporate social media links in your video descriptions. Make it easy for viewers to find and follow you on other platforms. A simple call-to-action at the end of your videos can encourage viewers to connect with you on social media, deepening their engagement with your channel.

Run social media ads. While not immediately necessary, investing in social media advertising can be a smart move once you've established your channel. Platforms like Facebook and Instagram offer targeted advertising options that can help you reach a wider, more specific audience.

Track your analytics. Just as with YouTube, analyzing your social media metrics can provide insights into what's working and what's not. Use this data to refine your strategy, experiment with new ideas, and ultimately, grow your audience.

Remember, leveraging social media for promotion isn't about overnight success. It's about consistent effort, strategic planning, and genuine engagement with your audience. With patience and perseverance, social media can become a powerful ally in growing your faceless YouTube channel.

Motivate your audience to share your content. When your viewers share your videos on their social media profiles, they're essentially vouching for your content to their friends and followers. Encourage sharing by creating relatable, share-worthy content and including call-to-actions that prompt viewers to share.

Finally, keep experimenting. Social media landscapes evolve rapidly. What works today might not work tomorrow, so stay agile. Keep an eye on trends, experiment with new platforms, and always be willing to adjust your strategy. Remember, every follower gained is a step closer to expanding your channel's reach and impact.

As you weave social media into your overall promotional strategy, you'll find it's more than just a platform for sharing content; it's a vibrant community eager to interact, engage, and support your journey. Harness the power of social media, and watch your faceless YouTube channel flourish.

Building a Community with Comments and Polls

When it comes to growing a faceless YouTube channel, engaging your audience isn't just a part of the journey; it's at the heart of what makes your channel thrive. You've crafted your videos with care and shared them with the world, but your job doesn't end when you hit "publish". It's time to roll up your sleeves and dive into the world of comments and polls.

Starting with comments, they're not just feedback; think of them as the lifeblood of your channel's community. Each comment is a direct line of communication with your viewers, offering invaluable insights into what they love about your content and where you can improve. But more than that, responding to comments creates a sense of connection. It shows that behind the faceless channel, there's a real person paying attention and valuing their audience's thoughts.

Here's a pro tip: don't just respond to the easy comments. Engage with the constructive criticism too, and even the occasional negative comment, with grace and professionalism. This approach not only helps maintain a positive environment but also builds your reputation as a respectful and attentive creator. Remember, every interaction in the comments section is a chance to reinforce the positive community you're building.

But it's not just about responding. It's also about initiating. Pose questions to your audience in your video or in the comment section itself. This encourages viewers to share their thoughts and experiences, leading to more engagement and a deeper connection with your community. It's this exchange of ideas that transforms passive viewers into active participants and loyal fans.

Moving on to polls, they are a goldmine for engagement and insights. YouTube's poll feature allows you to pose questions directly to your audience in the Community tab or even within a video itself. Polls are not just engaging; they're a powerful tool for understanding your audience's preferences and tailoring your content to their interests. Whether it's asking for feedback on video ideas or gathering opinions on hot topics related to your niche, each poll you create is an opportunity to make your viewers feel heard and valued.

Let's not forget the fun aspect. Polls can be a playful way to engage your audience, sparking excitement and anticipation about upcoming content or decisions. This interactive element adds a layer of community participation that can significantly boost viewer loyalty and time spent on your channel. It turns passive viewing into an interactive experience, making your audience more invested in your content.

Moreover, incorporating the results of polls and comments into your videos can further amplify this effect. When viewers see their input influencing your content, it reinforces their sense of belonging and investment in your channel's community. It's a win-win: your content becomes more attuned to your audience's preferences, and your viewers feel like active contributors to your channel's journey.

However, managing comments and polls effectively requires a strategy. Set aside time each day or week to engage with your audience. Use moderation tools to filter out spam or inappropriate comments, maintaining a positive space for genuine interaction. And always stay true to your channel's voice and vision; let your unique personality shine through in every reply and poll you create.

In this digital age, authenticity is key. Your audience can sense when interactions feel forced or disingenuous. So, whether it's through humorous responses, heartfelt thanks, or insightful replies, ensure that your engagement feels as real and authentic as the content you create. This authenticity is what will transform viewers into a dedicated community.

Another aspect to consider is the use of analytics. YouTube provides detailed metrics on engagement, including comments and poll responses. Dive into these numbers to understand what resonates with your audience. Notice trends in the types of comments or poll answers you receive, and use this data to fine-tune your engagement strategies and content planning.

Lastly, don't overlook the power of shoutouts and featured comments in fostering community spirit. Highlighting viewer comments in your videos or on social media not only makes those individuals feel special but also encourages more viewers to join the conversation, hoping to get noticed. It's a simple gesture that can significantly boost community engagement and loyalty.

Building a community around your faceless YouTube channel is both an art and a science. Comments and polls are tools at your disposal, waiting to be leveraged in creative and strategic ways. They invite interaction, provide valuable insights, and most importantly, forge a deeper connection with your audience.

To sum up, never underestimate the power of engaging your audience. Cherish every comment, relish in the insights from every poll, and always be on the lookout for new ways to connect and grow your community. After all, these aren't just viewers; they're the heartbeat of your channel. A vibrant, engaged community is the ultimate testament to a channel's success. So go ahead, invite your audience into the conversation, and watch your faceless channel flourish.

Collaborating with Other Creators

Let's dive right in. The journey of a faceless YouTube channel doesn't have to be a solo mission. In fact, one of the most dynamic ways to boost your channel's growth and engage more deeply with your audience is through collaborations with other creators. It's like throwing a party where everyone brings their own unique dish to the table—suddenly, you've got a feast. Collaborating isn't just about cross-promoting each other's work; it's about blending your talents to create something neither of you could have done on your own.

First off, identifying potential collaborators is your initial step. Look for creators who share your niche, or perhaps even those in complementary niches that can bring a new angle to your content. It's not just about subscriber count; it's about alignment. You're looking for creators whose quality of content, audience engagement, and creative vision match or enhance your own. Remember, a smaller channel with a highly engaged audience can sometimes be more valuable than a larger, less interactive channel.

After pinpointing who you'd like to collaborate with, reaching out is next. A personalized message works wonders—let them know why you think a collaboration would be mutually beneficial, and throw in some ideas about what you could create together. Be open-minded and flexible; it's a creative process that benefits from brainstorming and cooperation.

When you've got a collaboration in the works, planning is key. You're essentially merging two brands, albeit temporarily, so it's crucial to be on the same page about everything from the content's theme to the promotion strategy. Communicate clearly and set shared goals for what you both want to achieve with this partnership.

Creating the content itself should be fun! Whether you're blending your voices in a voiceover compilation, sharing screen space in a split-screen format, or guest starring on each other's channels, make sure the end product reflects the best of both worlds. It's this fusion of creativity that often leads to something truly special and engaging for the audience.

Promotion is where the magic happens. A collaboration is a chance to tap into each other's audiences, so don't be shy about sharing the content across all your social media platforms. Encourage your viewers to check out your collaborator's channel and vice versa. It's a win-win for both creators, with each of you gaining exposure to a wider audience.

Feedback and learning from the experience are just as important as the collaboration itself. After the video is live and the promotion has done its work, take time to analyze the results. How did your audience react? Did you see a bump in your subscriber count? What worked and what could be improved next time? This reflection is invaluable for honing your collaboration strategy moving forward.

Don't overlook the power of building a network. Even if a particular creator isn't a good fit for a direct collaboration, they might know someone who is. Networking within your niche can open up opportunities not just for collaborations but also for gaining insights into what others are doing to engage and grow their audience.

But what about the challenges? Yes, they exist—conflicting schedules, creative differences, and uneven contributions to the project can all crop up. It's how you navigate these issues that matters. Always approach collaborations with a spirit of partnership and openness to compromise. Clear, open communication from the get-go sets the foundation for a smooth collaboration.

The benefits of collaborating extend beyond a single video. It's about community building, both among creators and with your audience. When your viewers see you teaming up with another creator they respect, it strengthens their sense of community and can make your channel feel more connected to the wider digital ecosystem.

Encouraging audience crossover is another perk of successful collaborations. For fans of both channels, there's a thrill in seeing their favorite creators work together. It fosters a shared sense of community and encourages audience members to interact, blending fan bases in a way that benefits both creators.

Lastly, collaborations are a journey of growth. With each partnership, you'll refine your collaborative process, understand your audience better, and learn new ways to engage and entertain. Each collaboration teaches you more about creating content that resonates, not only with your existing audience but also with potential new followers.

Stepping out of your comfort zone to collaborate with other creators can seem daunting at first. But remember, the most successful YouTube channels are often those that are willing to innovate and experiment. Embrace the opportunity to create something unique, and who knows? You might just stumble upon your next viral hit.

As we wrap up this section, it's clear that collaborating with other creators is more than just a strategy; it's a mindset. It's about being open to new ideas, building relationships, and creating a space where creativity knows no bounds. So, reach out, connect, and start co-creating. The next chapter in your faceless YouTube channel's story could very well be a collaborative masterpiece waiting to happen.

In conclusion, collaboration is not just a powerful tool for growth and engagement; it's also a journey of discovery. Through partnership, you can unlock new levels of creativity, reach, and community building that can transform your faceless YouTube channel into a thriving hub of activity. So, let's collaborate and create something incredible together. Your audience—and your channel—will thank you for it.

Analyzing Audience Insights and Feedback

Right, let's talk about slicing through the vast ocean of data and feedback that YouTube throws at you. It's like panning for gold; you're sifting through to find those shiny nuggets of insight that could really take your channel to the next level. But, where do you start? Well, luckily, YouTube provides a pretty comprehensive analytics toolbox. Your job? Get cozy with it.

First off, understanding who's watching your content is crucial. Demographics can tell you a lot—age groups, geographical locations, viewing times. Why does this matter? Imagine you're creating highly engaging content for teenagers, but your analytics show most of your audience are adults. There's a mismatch you need to address. Either tweak your content to better suit your actual audience or adjust your promotional strategies to better reach your intended demographic.

Now, engagement metrics like watch time, likes, shares, and comments are pure gold. They give you a direct line to what's resonating with your audience. High engagement rates generally signal that your content is hitting the mark, encouraging YouTube's algorithms to push your videos to more viewers. Conversely, if certain videos have low engagement, it's a sign to reassess and adjust.

Feedback doesn't only come in numbers. Comments are a treasure trove of insights. Sure, you'll need to develop a thick skin—YouTube comments aren't always the most uplifting. However, constructive criticism, praise, questions, and even the occasional random thought can steer you towards what your audience craves, fears, and values. Engage with these comments, and you'll also be building a community, which is priceless.

Let's talk about the 'Audience Retention' graph. This is a fantastic tool for pinpointing exactly where viewers drop off or skip in your videos. If you notice a pattern where many viewers are leaving at a certain point, ask yourself why. Was there a sudden change in topic? Was the video too long? Identifying these moments can dramatically improve future content.

Trends are your friends. Keep an eye out for patterns in what content performs best. Is it a certain format, topic, or maybe a specific style of editing? Leveraging these insights can inform your content strategy, helping you produce more of what works and less of what doesn't.

Comparing your channel's performance isn't just about looking inward. Analyze what your competitors are doing right (or wrong). This doesn't mean copycatting, but rather, seeking inspiration and understanding trends within your niche. Maybe there's an underserved segment within your niche that you could capture.

YouTube Studio's 'Audience' tab also gives you insights into what other videos your audience watches, which can be a fantastic way to discover new collaboration opportunities or content ideas. It's like uncovering your viewers' other love affairs with content and figuring out how your channel can be the main squeeze.

Don't overlook the power of polls and community posts. They are direct lines to your audience's preferences and thoughts. A quick poll can offer you instant feedback on what your subscribers are interested in, guiding your next content move.

Integration with social media platforms can provide additional layers of feedback. Seeing how your content performs across different platforms can give you insights into where your content might be more suited or more popular. Spread your presence and listen to the feedback from these different venues too.

Setting measurable goals based on your insights is crucial. Maybe it's increasing your average watch time by a certain percentage or improving your like-to-dislike ratio. Use these insights as benchmarks for your success and continuously strive to exceed them with each content rollout.

Remember, data and feedback analysis is a continuous process. The digital landscape shifts quickly, and staying on top of these changes is what can keep your channel growing. Make a habit of regular check-ins with your analytics.

Also, consider the 'why' behind the data. It's not just about understanding what is happening, but why it's happening. This deeper level of insight will enable you to make more informed strategic decisions, aligning your content creation more closely with your audience's wants and needs.

Finally, never lose sight of the bigger picture. Each piece of data, each comment, each like, and dislike, they all contribute to your journey.

Do not get so caught up in optimizing and tweaking based on feedback that you lose your channel's unique voice.

Analyzing audience insights and feedback isn't just about bettering your content; it's about creating a dialogue with your viewers, understanding them on a deeper level, and, ultimately, crafting a community that thrives together. So, dive into those analytics, read those comments, and keep pushing your content to new heights. The insights you gain today will be the foundation of your channel's growth tomorrow.

Chapter 8

Monetization Strategies

Now that we've got the ball rolling with setting up and growing your channel, it's time to dive into the meaty part – making that sweet, sweet passive income! Monetizing your content isn't just about slapping ads on your videos and waiting for the money to roll in. It's about smartly leveraging multiple revenue streams to maximize your earnings. From joining the YouTube Partner Program, which is your ticket to earning ad revenue and tapping into YouTube Premium earnings, to exploring affiliate marketing, sponsorships, and those juicy brand deals, there are plenty of avenues to explore. And let's not forget about selling your own digital products and merchandise. This is where your creativity and understanding of your audience turn into cold hard cash. Each of these strategies has its own set of tricks and tips to truly make them work for you, and that's what we're here to decode. By diversifying your revenue streams, you'll not only bulletproof your income but also increase your channel's value to sponsors and advertisers. So, let's get into the nitty-gritty of turning your faceless YouTube channel into a money-making machine.

Joining the YouTube Partner Program

So, you've set up your channel, started creating awesome content, and now you're thinking, "How do I start making some real dough out of this?" Well, entering the YouTube Partner Program (YPP) is a significant first step towards monetizing your faceless channel. Let's dive into what this means and how you can get there.

The YouTube Partner Program isn't just a status symbol; it's a gateway to various monetization features such as ad revenue, Super Chat, Channel Memberships, and more. But, like any exclusive club, there are a few hurdles you need to jump over first.

Firstly, you need to hit YouTube's eligibility requirements: 1,000 subscribers and 4,000 watch hours over the past 12 months. It might sound like scaling a mountain, but with consistent, quality content, it's entirely achievable. Focus on creating videos that provide value, whether that's through entertainment, education, or inspiration, and your audience will grow.

Next up, ensure your channel adheres to all of YouTube's policies and guidelines. This might sound like a no-brainer, but you'd be surprised how many people slip up here. Make sure your content is original, or if you're using third-party content, you have the necessary rights or it falls under fair use. YouTube takes this very seriously, so don't skip this step.

Assuming you've got all that in place, you'll then need to sign up for AdSense or link an existing AdSense account to your YouTube account. This is how YouTube will pay you, so ensure all your information is accurate and up-to-date.

Once you've applied to the YPP, patience is key. It can take a while for YouTube to review your application, but as long as you're following the rules and creating engaging content, you'll get there.

But joining the YPP is just the start. To make the most out of your partnership, you'll want to optimize your videos for ad revenue. This could mean thinking about placement of ads within your video, considering what type of ads are best suited for your content, and even strategizing your video's length to maximize earning potential.

Don't put all your eggs in one basket, though. The most successful YouTubers diversify their income streams. While ad revenue can be significant, exploring other avenues within YPP like Channel Memberships or Super Chat during live streams can really boost your income.

Engage with your audience to make these features work for you. For instance, exclusive content for channel members can create a sense of community and exclusivity. Meanwhile, acknowledging contributors on Super Chat during live streams can encourage more viewers to participate.

Remember, the YouTube Partner Program is a partnership. YouTube provides the platform and tools, but it's up to you to create content that attracts and retains an audience. It's about creating a symbiotic relationship where both parties benefit.

It's also worth noting that the digital landscape is always changing. Keeping abreast of new monetization features and strategies within YPP will ensure you're always maximizing your earning potential.

Moreover, don't get discouraged if progress seems slow at first. Many successful YouTubers didn't see significant earnings until they'd been at it for a while. Persistence, creativity, and engagement with your audience will pay off in the long run.

Lastly, remember that monetizing your channel isn't just about making money—it's about building a sustainable business. This means being strategic about your content, understanding your audience, and staying true to your brand. When done right, joining the YouTube Partner Program is just the beginning of a rewarding journey.

So, keep pushing forward, keep refining your craft, and let your passion drive you. The YouTube Partner Program is an excellent opportunity for faceless channels to thrive and establish themselves in the vast digital ocean of content. With dedication and strategy, you can turn your channel into a vibrant community and a lucrative business.

Embrace the journey, enjoy the process, and look forward to the rewards. The road to joining the YouTube Partner Program and succeeding within it is challenging but incredibly fulfilling. Welcome to the next chapter of your YouTube career!

Exploring Ad Revenue and YouTube Premium

So, you've got your faceless YouTube channel up and running. It's time to talk about turning those views into cash. You might think it's too soon, but trust me, understanding how to monetize your content from the get-go can supercharge your motivation. Let's dive into ad revenue and YouTube Premium, two pivotal elements of your monetization strategy.

First up, ad revenue. It's the bread and butter for many YouTubers. Once you're part of the YouTube Partner Program, you'll start earning money every time someone watches or clicks on the ads shown in your videos. But here's the catch – not all ads are created equal. The amount you earn can vary massively based on your niche, audience location, and even the time of year.

To maximize your ad revenue, you need to understand what appeals to advertisers. They love high-engagement, family-friendly content that keeps viewers watching. Why? Because it gives their ads the best chance of being seen and acted upon. So, when planning your content, think about what will keep your audience hooked while staying advertiser-friendly.

But don't get too hung up on chasing ad revenue alone. It's important, yes, but it's also unpredictable. That's where YouTube Premium comes in, offering a more stable income stream. Premium subscribers pay a monthly fee to enjoy ad-free viewing, and creators get a slice of that pie based on how much Premium members watch their content.

The beauty of YouTube Premium revenue is that it's not based on ads. Instead, it focuses on viewer engagement. The more engaging your content, the longer Premium subscribers will watch, increasing your earnings. It's a great incentive to focus on quality and engagement in your video content.

But how do you get started? Well, both these revenue streams become accessible once you're a part of the YouTube Partner Program, which requires your channel to have at least 1,000 subscribers and 4,000 watch hours over the last 12 months. It might sound like a steep hill, but with consistent, high-quality content, you'll get there before you know it.

Once you're in the program, it's all about optimizing your content for both ad revenue and YouTube Premium. For ads, you'll want to play around with different formats – like skippable video ads, non-skippable video ads, and bumper ads – to see what works best for your content and audience. Remember, the key is to enhance your earnings without compromising the viewer's experience.

And when it comes to YouTube Premium, focus on creating content that people can't just walk away from. Long-form videos that keep viewers hooked, interesting series that encourage binge-watching, and evergreen content that draws in viewers over time are especially effective.

Let's not forget about CPM (Cost Per Mille), or the amount you earn per thousand views. Different niches can have wildly different CPM rates. If you're in a lucrative niche like finance or technology, you could see higher earnings per view. But remember, chasing a niche just for the high CPM can backfire if you're not genuinely interested in the topic. Authenticity is key to long-term success on YouTube.

Also, keep in mind that YouTube ad revenue can fluctuate. Factors like changes in viewer behavior, shifts in advertising spending, and updates to YouTube's algorithms can all affect your earnings. That's why diversifying your income streams, which we'll discuss in other sections, is so crucial.

For those worried about creating content that aligns with YouTube's ad policies, there's good news. YouTube provides resources and guidelines to help creators understand what's considered advertiser-friendly. They also offer features like self-certification and the ability to appeal demonetization decisions, giving creators more control over their monetization status.

Now, a word of encouragement. Every successful YouTuber started with zero subscribers and zero views. The path to monetization might seem long and challenging, but it's filled with opportunities to learn, grow, and, eventually, earn. Stay focused on creating valuable and engaging content, and the rest will follow.

Finally, let's talk strategy. Balancing your content to appeal to both advertisers and your audience can seem like a tightrope walk. But it's possible. Your goal should be to create a content strategy that aligns with your passions, meets YouTube's guidelines, and delivers value to your audience. This balance is the key to unlocking both ad revenue and YouTube Premium earnings.

In conclusion, understanding and leveraging ad revenue and YouTube Premium are critical steps in your journey to monetizing your faceless YouTube channel. Focus on creating engaging, high-quality content that appeals to viewers and advertisers alike. Keep your eyes on the prize, and remember, every view, every subscriber, and every dollar earned is a step forward in your creator journey. The road to monetization is a journey worth taking, and you've got what it takes to make it happen.

Affiliate Marketing, Sponsorships, and Brand Deals

Creeping into the heart of monetization strategies for faceless YouTube channels, we tap into a realm ripe with potential: Affiliate marketing, sponsorships, and brand deals. This trio of opportunities can transform your channel from a hobby into a robust revenue stream. But how do you navigate this landscape? Let's break it down and create a roadmap to success.

First off, affiliate marketing. Think of it as earning a commission by promoting products or services. You don't need to own the product, which perfectly suits the faceless channel model. You simply share a unique affiliate link in your video descriptions. When your viewers click through and make a purchase, you get a piece of the pie. The beauty of affiliate marketing is its scalability. You can start small, recommending products you genuinely love and use, and gradually expand your affiliations as your audience grows.

It's crucial, however, to maintain transparency with your audience. Trust is paramount. Clearly disclose your affiliate partnerships, ensuring your viewers are informed. The trust you build can convert into loyalty and increased conversions, fostering a win-win scenario for you and your audience.

Moving on to sponsorships. This is where companies pay you to create content that promotes their products or services. This could range from a dedicated product review to subtly incorporating the product into your regular content. The key to securing sponsorships is to have a well-defined target audience. Brands are looking for creators who can effectively reach and engage potential customers on their behalf.

Creating a media kit can set you apart. This document showcases your audience demographics, engagement statistics, and notable achievements. It's your pitch deck to potential sponsors, proving the value you can bring to their marketing efforts.

But don't wait for brands to find you. Be proactive. Reach out to brands that align with your channel's values and content. Tailor each pitch to the specific brand, demonstrating how a partnership could be mutually beneficial. The right fit can lead to long-term collaborations that add significant value to your channel and to the brand.

Now, let's talk brand deals. Similar to sponsorships but typically on a larger scale, brand deals involve collaborations where you partner with companies for comprehensive campaigns. This might include a series of videos, social media mentions, and even appearances at events. Landing brand deals requires a significant following and a track record of successful partnerships, but it's definitely a goal worth aspiring to.

Negotiation is part of the game. Remember, your platform offers valuable access to a dedicated audience. Don't sell yourself short. Understand your worth and negotiate accordingly, while being open to creative compensation packages. Sometimes, the best deals are a mix of upfront payment, commission on sales, and free products or services.

As you explore these avenues, diversification is your best strategy. Don't put all your eggs in one basket. Success in YouTube monetization often comes from multiple streams of income. Affiliate sales, sponsorships, and brand deals each have their cycles and seasons. By diversifying, you create a more stable and sustainable income.

Stay informed about the products and trends within your niche. This knowledge not only informs your content creation but also makes you a more attractive partner to brands. Companies look for creators who are authorities in their space. Your expertise can position you as the ideal collaborator for brands looking to connect with engaged audiences.

Timing can also play a crucial role. Be strategic about when you pitch to brands or promote affiliate products. Aligning your content with key shopping periods, such as the holiday season or back-to-school, can amplify your earnings. Capitalizing on these times can significantly increase your affiliate income and attractiveness to potential sponsors.

Finally, patience is essential. Building a profitable channel through affiliate marketing, sponsorships, and brand deals doesn't happen overnight. It requires consistent effort and content of value. Keep focusing on creating great content and growing your audience. As your platform expands, so will your monetization opportunities.

In the end, integrity is your most valuable asset. Stay true to your values and only promote products or engage in partnerships that you believe in. Your audience's trust is the foundation of your channel's success. Protect it fiercely.

Embrace the journey of monetizing your faceless YouTube channel with excitement and determination. There's a world of opportunity waiting for creators who are ready to explore and innovate. Your channel has the potential to not only entertain and inform but also to thrive financially through affiliate marketing, sponsorships, and brand deals. Let your passion lead the way, and the revenue will follow.

Remember, success is not only about how much money you make but also about the impact you have on your audience and the authenticity of your brand partnerships. Stay focused, stay driven, and watch as your channel transforms into a significant income source, powered by strategic partnerships and savvy marketing moves.

Selling Digital Products and Merchandise

Entering the realm of monetization through your faceless YouTube channel, you're essentially stepping onto a platform that's ripe with potential. Selling digital products and merchandise isn't just a side gig; it's a major revenue avenue, turning your channel into a multifaceted business. Here's a deep dive into turning your content and brand into tangible earnings through digital products and physical merchandise. It's simpler than you think, and with a bit of creativity and strategic planning, you could see a substantial increase in your income.

Firstly, understanding the power of digital products is crucial. E-books, courses, downloads, and licenses are just the tip of the iceberg. Picture this: you've built a dedicated audience who trusts your voice and expertise. Offering them more in-depth information or tools through digital products not only broadens your revenue streams but also deepens the connection with your audience. It's about offering value that complements your video content, creating a full-circle content experience for your audience.

Creating digital products might seem like a leap, but it aligns closely with content creation. If you're educating your audience on specific topics, why not compile an e-book or an online course? This not only cements your authority in your niche but leverages your content to work double-time for your income. Start small, listen to your audience's needs, and build from there. The feedback loop you create will be invaluable as you refine and expand your offerings.

Onto merchandise, the personal touch it brings can't be overstated. Merchandise transforms viewers into walking billboards for your brand. But more than that, it allows your audience to own a piece of the community you've built together. Whether it's apparel, accessories, or lifestyle products, the key is quality and design that resonates with your brand's ethos. This isn't just about slapping your logo on a mug; it's about creating items people are excited to use and wear.

The logistics of selling merchandise can intimidate creators, but third-party platforms have made it simpler than ever. With print-on-demand services, you hold no inventory, minimizing risk and investment. These platforms integrate directly with your social media and websites, automating the process. It's a game-changer, offering a seamless transition from content creator to brand owner.

Tapping into audience insights will guide your decisions in both digital and physical product offerings. What content resonates the most? Can you expand it into an informative course or a line of merchandise? Engaging with your audience through polls and direct communication will not only provide you with ideas but also create anticipation for your products.

Pricing strategy plays a pivotal role in ensuring your products are accessible yet profitable. Research your industry standards but consider the unique value you're providing. A well-defined pricing structure that factors in production costs, platform fees, and your profit margin will ensure your venture into merchandise and digital products is sustainable.

Marketing your products should be an extension of your regular content strategy. Innovative ways to showcase your merchandise or digital products within your videos can act as natural endorsements. Creating specific content that highlights the value of your offerings can pique interest and drive sales. Remember, consistency in branding across your YouTube channel, digital products, and merchandise cements a cohesive brand image in your audience's mind.

Collaborations can amplify your reach and introduce your products to new audiences. Partnering with fellow creators or brands for limited edition merchandise or bundled digital products can create buzz and enhance the perceived value of your offerings.

Coupons and limited-time offers are powerful incentives that can drive immediate action. Launching new products with special deals for your most loyal subscribers rewards their dedication and can increase early sales, creating momentum.

Don't underestimate the power of social proof. Sharing testimonials, user-generated content, and featuring customer reviews can significantly influence buying decisions. Highlighting the community around your merchandise or digital products makes potential buyers feel like they're purchasing more than just an item—they're joining a movement.

Handling customer service with care ensures your venture into selling products is met with satisfaction, securing repeat customers and fostering brand loyalty. A satisfied customer is more likely to buy again and spread the word. Streamline the purchasing process, be transparent about shipping and handling times, and handle inquiries and issues promptly and gracefully.

Lastly, analyzing the performance of your products is vital for long-term success. Which items are your bestsellers? What marketing strategies drove the most sales? Use analytics to your advantage, tweaking your approach based on concrete data. This will help you refine your offerings and marketing strategies, increasing your profitability over time.

Expanding into the sale of digital products and merchandise is a natural extension of the hard work you've put into building your faceless YouTube channel. It's about leveraging the audience you've built and offering them more ways to engage with your brand. With thoughtful planning, quality products, and strategic marketing, you can significantly boost your income and create a more robust, resilient business. Remember, each step forward expands your brand beyond the screen, turning your creative passion into a thriving, diversified income source.

Take the leap, trust in your brand, and remember: your unique voice and content have already built a community. Offering digital products and merchandise is just another way to grow with and serve your audience better. It's more than just an income stream; it's a way to deepen connections, affirm your brand, and take your YouTube venture to new heights.

Chapter 9

Creating Passive Income Streams

Now that we've delved into the nuts and bolts of launching and monetizing your faceless YouTube channel, let's pivot to a topic that gets everyone excited: creating passive income streams. Imagine making money while you sleep, travel, or work on new projects. That's the beauty of passive income—it keeps flowing in once the groundwork has been laid. In this chapter, we're going to explore several avenues for setting up automated revenue models that can help you achieve just that. Whether it's through licensing your content so others can use it or syndicating your videos across different platforms for broader reach and additional income, the opportunities are vast. We'll also touch on how investing in other business opportunities or scaling up by managing multiple channels can substantially increase your earnings without multiplying your workload. Remember, the goal isn't to create more work for yourself, but to work smarter. By diversifying your income sources and setting up systems that generate revenue on autopilot, you're not just earning money—you're building long-term wealth and freeing up your most precious resource: time.

Setting Up Automated Revenue Models

Gearing up for financial success on YouTube isn't just about producing content consistently. It's about smartly aligning your work with revenue models that earn you money while you sleep. In this chapter, we're diving deep into how you can set up automated revenue streams for your faceless YouTube channel. This approach is not just about adding income sources; it's about creating a strategy that ensures continuous cash flow with minimal ongoing effort.

To start, let's talk about the YouTube Partner Program (YPP). Once you're in, ads play on your videos, and you get a cut. It sounds simple, but the trick is in optimizing your videos for maximum ad revenue. This includes understanding the types of ads that generate the most income and strategically placing them in your video content.

Next up is affiliate marketing. This is where you promote products or services and earn a commission for sales made through your links. The beauty of affiliate marketing? It integrates seamlessly with your content. For instance, if you run a tech review channel, linking to the gadgets you review can earn you significant commissions without altering the viewer's experience.

Let's not forget about sponsorships. While not entirely passive, once set up, long-term sponsorship deals can provide steady income over time. The key is to create packages that offer continued value to the sponsor, making it easy to renew contracts or attract similar deals.

Digital products are another gold mine for passive income. Think eBooks, courses, or even preset packs for photography. The effort is upfront in creating the product, but once it's live, it can sell indefinitely with the right promotion through your videos and community engagement.

Speaking of community, launching a membership program on platforms like Patreon offers your audience exclusive content for a fee. While it does require regular updates, the model establishes a direct revenue line from your most dedicated fans.

But how do you keep all these revenue streams flowing without getting overwhelmed? Automation and delegation are your friends here. Tools like social media schedulers, email marketing software, and even hiring a virtual assistant can help manage the day-to-day tasks, leaving you more time to create or strategize.

Analytics play a crucial role too. By regularly reviewing your revenue performance across different streams, you can identify what's working and what's not. This data allows you to pivot or double down on strategies to maximize income.

Now, consider the power of licensing your content. Platforms and media outlets are always on the lookout for quality video content. By licensing your videos, you tap into an additional revenue source without extra work on previously created content.

Also, think about repurposing your content across platforms. A video on YouTube could become a podcast episode, a blog post, or even a series of Instagram Stories. Each platform offers additional monetization opportunities, amplifying your earning potential from the same piece of content.

For those ready to explore investments, the revenue from your YouTube channel can serve as capital. Investing in stocks, real estate, or even other digital assets can diversify your income, ensuring you're not solely reliant on YouTube.

But what about scalability? As your channel grows, expanding your brand into merchandise can offer both brand strengthening and a new revenue stream. Services like Teespring integrate directly with YouTube, making it easier than ever to offer branded merchandise to your viewers.

Finally, recognize the power of your brand. As your channel gains visibility, opportunities for cross-promotion and partnerships increase. These can offer substantial one-time payments or ongoing revenue opportunities.

In conclusion, setting up automated revenue models requires a mix of strategy, creativity, and a bit of upfront work. However, once in place, these models can ensure a steady flow of income, freeing you up to focus on content creation and growth. Remember, the goal is to work smarter, not harder, turning your faceless YouTube channel into a thriving, financially successful enterprise.

As you embark on this journey, stay patient and persistent. Success in monetization doesn't happen overnight, but with dedication and the right strategies, you can create a sustainable and lucrative income stream from your faceless YouTube channel. Keep experimenting, keep learning, and most importantly, keep creating. Your financial freedom might just be a few strategic moves away.

Licensing and Syndicating Content

So you've created some killer content, and it's starting to pick up steam. Now, what if I told you there's a way to squeeze even more value out of those videos with minimal effort on your part? Enter the world of licensing and syndicating content. This is where you allow others to use your content, either as is or in a modified form, in exchange for a fee or a share of the revenue. Sounds pretty sweet, right?

Licensing content is straightforward. You retain ownership of your videos, but you give someone else permission to use them. This could be a TV network, an educational platform, or another digital content provider. They get quality content to share with their audience, and you get a new income stream. It's a win-win.

Then there's syndication. This is slightly different and usually involves a third party distributing your content across multiple platforms. This can massively increase your reach and expose your brand to audiences you might not have tapped into yet.

Now, why bother with all this? First, it's passive income. Once you've created the content and struck a deal, the money comes in whether you're working or not. Second, it amplifies your reach and reputation. Every time someone sees your content on a platform outside of YouTube, that's more potential subscribers and more influence in your niche.

Getting started might seem daunting, but it's all about making connections. Start by putting yourself out there. Attend industry events, network with content distributors, and join online communities related to your niche. The goal is to get your content and your name in front of the people who can help you syndicate or license it.

When it comes to the nitty-gritty of licensing deals, transparency and clear agreements are key. Ensure that the terms of any deal - from fees to how the content can be used - are spelled out in a contract. This protects you and ensures that your content isn't misused.

If you're looking into syndication, research third-party platforms that specialize in distributing online video content. Some platforms take a cut of your revenue in exchange for their services, while others might charge upfront. Weigh the costs against the potential reach and revenue to see if it's worth it for you.

Digital content platforms like Roku or Amazon Prime could be great places to start. They constantly need fresh content and have vast audiences willing to consume it. Plus, having your content featured on a recognizable platform can massively boost your brand's credibility.

Don't forget about niche platforms either. Depending on your content's topic, there might be smaller, specialized platforms where your videos could stand out more. These specialized audiences can be incredibly engaged and loyal, leading to higher per-view earnings than you might get on more generalized platforms.

However, licensing and syndicating content isn't a set-it-and-forget-it deal. You need to monitor where and how your content is being used. Regularly review your licensing agreements and syndication performance. Is your content reaching the right audiences? Are you being compensated fairly based on the terms of your contracts?

Inevitably, as your content starts circulating more widely, you'll encounter challenges. You might have to deal with copyright issues or negotiate better terms as your brand grows. That's why it's crucial to have a good attorney who knows the digital media landscape to help navigate these waters.

Moreover, consider the long-term potential. As your channel grows, so does the value of your content library. Start thinking about your content not just as individual videos but as a valuable asset that can continuously generate income over time.

Remember, licensing and syndicating content is all about leveraging what you've already created. It's like having an investment property; with the right management, it can provide ongoing returns with relatively little additional input from you.

So, don't let your content just sit there. By exploring licensing and syndication opportunities, you can unlock new revenue streams, reach broader audiences, and take your brand to new heights. The digital world is vast, and the potential for your content is limited only by your willingness to explore it.

Inspiration is good, but action is better. Start mapping out a plan to push your content beyond YouTube. Research potential partners, reach out to platforms, and maybe even consider a consultation with a media distribution specialist. Your content has power; it's time to maximize it.

The journey to creating passive income through your faceless YouTube channel is exciting and filled with opportunities. Licensing and syndicating your content is a key part of that journey. It's not just about making more money; it's about growing your brand and making your mark on the world. So go ahead, take that step, and watch your channel flourish in ways you never imagined.

Investing in Other Business Opportunities

After nailing down the art of creating and monetizing faceless YouTube channels, you might find yourself with a bit more cash flow and a lot more confidence. What's next? For many creators, the logical next step is to diversify and invest in other business opportunities. But where to start, you might wonder. Let's dive into some actionable strategies that can further bolster your passive income streams and expand your entrepreneurial empire.

First off, understand that branching out doesn't mean stepping away from what has made you successful. Instead, think of this as enhancing your existing portfolio. Investing in areas related to your channel's niche could be a brilliant move. If you've been running a successful cooking channel, for instance, consider developing a line of kitchen products or even investing in food startups. This way, your brand and your business grow hand in hand, each supporting the other.

Don't limit yourself to products either. Digital products and services offer tremendous potential for passive income. Online courses, e-books, and paid membership sites can generate revenue long after the initial effort of creating them. Leverage the audience you've built on YouTube to sell these products effectively. Remember, you've already earned their trust, making them more likely to support your new ventures.

Real estate is another avenue worth exploring. With a relatively stable and passive income, real estate investments can supplement your digital earnings significantly. You don't have to dive in headfirst; start small with rental properties or consider real estate investment trusts (REITs) if you're not ready for direct ownership. The key is to make your money work for you, even while you sleep.

Then there's the stock market. It might seem daunting at first, but with a little education and patience, investing in stocks can be a lucrative way to build wealth. Focus on long-term investments in companies you believe in, rather than trying to time the market for quick gains. There are plenty of resources out there to get you started, including online courses and investment apps that make trading more accessible than ever.

Don't forget about partnerships with fellow creators or entrepreneurs. These can open doors to new projects and investment opportunities you might not have found on your own. Plus, working with someone means sharing the risks and the rewards, making it a less daunting venture into new territory.

Franchising is another path to consider. It involves a bigger upfront investment and a lot of hard work, but owning a franchise of an established brand can be extremely rewarding. It's a way to own a business without having to build everything from the ground up, benefiting from the brand's existing reputation and operational support.

Peer-to-peer lending platforms present an opportunity to earn interest on your capital by loaning it out to individuals or small businesses. It's a more hands-on investment, requiring you to assess risk and choose your borrowers carefully, but it can yield higher returns than traditional savings or investment options.

E-commerce is booming, and setting up an online store to sell products can tap into the global marketplace. Platforms like Shopify make it easier than ever to create a store, sell products, and even dropship items without ever handling them yourself. It's a fantastic way to build a brand and sell products directly to the consumer.

Investing in startups is a higher risk but potentially high reward venture. If you have a keen eye for innovation and aren't afraid to bet on the future, this could be right up your alley. Platforms like AngelList have democratized access to startup investments, giving you the chance to get in on the ground floor of the next big thing.

Remember, investing is a marathon, not a sprint. It's important to do your research, understand the risks involved, and never invest more than you can afford to lose. Diversification is key to building a robust investment portfolio that can withstand market fluctuations and provide steady growth over time.

Maintain a learning mindset. The world of investment and business opportunities is ever-changing, and there's always something new to discover. Subscribe to financial newsletters, listen to investment podcasts, and join online communities of entrepreneurs to stay informed and inspired.

Consider investing in personal development as well. Courses in financial literacy, business management, or even public speaking can enhance your skills and open up new opportunities. The investment you make in yourself is often the most rewarding one, paying dividends in all areas of your life.

Finally, don't be afraid to seek professional advice. Whether it's a financial advisor, a mentor in your field, or a business coach, having expert guidance can help you make informed decisions and avoid common pitfalls. Investing in other business opportunities is an exciting path to financial freedom, but it's wise to have a helping hand along the way.

Embarking on this journey beyond YouTube might be the most challenging thing you've ever done, but it can also be the most rewarding. With strategic planning, a bit of courage, and a willingness to learn from both successes and failures, you can build a diverse portfolio of passive income streams that will support your dreams for years to come. So, what are you waiting for? The next big opportunity might be just around the corner, waiting for you to seize it.

Scaling Up with Multiple Channels

Imagine you've crafted a faceless YouTube channel that's buzzing with activity, generating income while you sleep. It's thrilling, right? Now, what if you could multiply that success? That's where the magic of scaling up with multiple channels comes into play. It's about taking the blueprint that worked for you once and replicating it to amplify your earnings and impact.

First things first, understand that managing multiple channels isn't just about duplicating content across several platforms. It's about strategically diversifying your presence to capture various audience segments. Each channel you create or acquire should cater to a distinct niche or interest group. This way, you're not putting all your eggs in one basket but spreading your risk and potential for reward across a broader landscape.

Beyond diversification, scaling up offers the advantage of cross-promotion. You can leverage the audience from one channel to boost another by sharing relevant content across your channels. This not just maximizes your reach but also fosters a stronger community across your network of channels.

Now, you might be pondering, "How do I manage the workload?" It's a valid concern. The key is in building systems and teams. Initially, you could be the jack-of-all-trades for your first channel, but as you scale, delegating tasks becomes crucial. Hiring freelance editors, scriptwriters, and voiceover artists or even building a small team can streamline your content production process, making scaling up feasible and less daunting.

Another crucial aspect of managing multiple channels is maintaining a consistent quality and brand voice across all platforms. Your audience should feel a seamless connection between your channels, even if they cater to different niches. Consistency in production value, storytelling approach, and engaging content will keep your viewers hooked, regardless of the channel they are watching.

Financial management also plays a pivotal role in scaling up. It's important to reinvest profits from your channels back into your growing empire. Whether it's through upgrading equipment, investing in advertising, or hiring talent, wise reinvestment can fuel your channels' growth and help you scale up more efficiently.

Don't forget the power of analytics. Keeping a close eye on the performance of each channel will help you understand what works and what doesn't, enabling you to make informed decisions about where to allocate resources most effectively. Tools like YouTube Analytics provide a wealth of data that can guide your strategy as you scale.

Scaling up with multiple channels also means more opportunities for monetization. From ad revenue and affiliate marketing to sponsorships and merchandise sales, having several channels creates multiple revenue streams. This diversification not only increases your potential income but also safeguards you against fluctuations in market trends or advertising rates.

Networking and collaborations become even more beneficial when you operate multiple channels. By establishing partnerships with other creators, you can tap into new audiences, share valuable insights, and even share the workload of content creation. A collaborative approach can significantly amplify your growth and reach.

Risks are an inherent part of scaling up, and it's crucial to approach this expansion with a strategic mindset. Be prepared for the increased workload and potential challenges that come with managing multiple channels. It's important to stay organized, keep a close eye on the market, and be adaptable to changes in your niche or YouTube's algorithm.

Encouragingly, technology and software solutions have made it easier than ever to manage multiple channels. From scheduling tools to analytics dashboards, there are numerous resources available to help streamline your operations and keep your content consistent across all channels.

Remember, patience is a virtue in the world of YouTube. Growing a single channel takes time and effort, and scaling up to multiple channels multiplies this commitment. Don't expect overnight success; instead, focus on building a solid foundation for each channel, nurturing your audience, and gradually expanding your digital empire.

Finally, let's not lose sight of the ultimate goal: building passive income streams. While scaling up with multiple channels can significantly increase your workload initially, the long-term payoff can be immense. With time, you'll refine your systems, build a dedicated team, and enjoy the fruits of your labor as your channels collectively contribute to a substantial, steady income.

Embarking on the journey of scaling up your faceless YouTube channel empire is both an exciting and complex endeavor. It requires diligence, strategic planning, and a pinch of creativity. However, with the right mindset and approach, you can transform your initial success into a sprawling network of profitable channels, each serving as a vital component of your overall passive income strategy. Stay focused, be patient, and persistently pursue excellence. The digital landscape is vast, and the opportunities for growth are limitless. Dive in, scale up, and witness your passive income streams multiply before your eyes.

Chapter 10

Staying Ahead of the Curve

Just when you think you've got it all figured out, YouTube goes ahead and changes the game. That's why in this hustle, staying ahead of the curve isn't just smart; it's essential. Let's dig into how you can be that savvy Youtuber who's always a couple of steps ahead. Adapting to YouTube's algorithm changes means keeping your ear to the ground, always ready to tweak and refine your strategy based on solid data, not just hunches. Experimenting with new content formats could be your golden ticket. Ever tried integrating YouTube Shorts into your content mix? It's a game-changer, offering a fresh way to hook viewers and boost your channel's visibility. And don't even get me started on the untapped potential in harnessing the power of emerging trends and opportunities. Imagine hitting the sweet spot with a format or topic no one else has thought of yet. So, get creative, stay flexible, and remember: being at the top of your game means never getting too comfortable. Keep pushing boundaries, and you might just be the next big thing on YouTube.

Adapting to YouTube Algorithm Changes

The ever-evolving nature of YouTube's algorithm can be both a blessing and a curse for creators. It's designed to keep the platform fresh and engaging for viewers, but it can be a real headache for channel owners trying to keep up. The key to mastering this ever-changing beast lies in adopting a flexible, forward-thinking approach to your content strategy.

First things first, it's crucial to stay informed. YouTube occasionally shares updates about major changes to its algorithm and how it affects video distribution. These updates often come through official YouTube blogs and forums. Making a habit of checking these resources can give you a head start in adapting your strategy to meet the new standards.

Engagement metrics play a colossal role in how your videos are ranked and recommended by the algorithm. It's not just about views anymore. Watch time, likes, comments, and the number of shares your video generates are all critical factors. Encouraging your viewers to interact with your content is more important than ever. This means creating videos that foster a sense of community and conversation among your audience.

Consistency is another pillar of success on YouTube. However, with the algorithm's penchant for novelty, how do you balance consistency with innovation? The answer lies in diversification within your niche. Keep your core content steady while experimenting with new themes or formats that could appeal to your audience. This keeps your channel fresh and gives you data on what new directions might be worth exploring further.

SEO isn't just for Google. YouTube's search function operates on a similar principle, prioritizing content based on keyword relevance, engagement metrics, and content quality. Continual optimization of your video titles, descriptions, and tags is necessary to ensure your content remains discoverable. Keep abreast of changes in search behavior and update your keywords accordingly.

Another facet of the YouTube algorithm is its recommendation system. YouTube aims to keep users on the platform as long as possible by recommending videos that they are likely to watch next. This means that creating videos that can easily be linked to each other through playlists or themes can increase the chances of your content being recommended after similar videos.

User feedback through comments and likes/dislikes provides direct indicators of your content's performance. Paying close attention to viewer feedback can offer actionable insights into what's working and what isn't. This direct line of communication with your audience is a valuable tool for adapting your content strategy to better suit their preferences.

Don't put all your eggs in one basket. With the algorithm's fickleness, diversifying your content across different platforms can safeguard your audience reach. Platforms like Instagram, Twitter, and even TikTok can support your YouTube channel by driving traffic and increasing engagement.

Collaborations can be a goldmine for growth, especially when navigating through changes in the algorithm. Teaming up with fellow creators can introduce your channel to new audiences, enhance content quality, and stimulate viewer engagement across multiple channels.

Investing time in analytics is non-negotiable. YouTube provides a wealth of data through its analytics dashboard, where you can track everything from viewer demographics to engagement metrics in real-time. This information is invaluable for identifying trends, monitoring the performance of your content, and making informed decisions on future content.

Innovation is key to staying ahead of the curve. Experiment with new video formats, storytelling techniques, and content ideas. YouTube forwards motion, so creators who are willing to adapt and innovate tend to find favor with the algorithm. Plus, experimenting keeps your channel dynamic and engaging for your audience.

Remember, coping with algorithm changes isn't a one-size-fits-all scenario. What works for one channel might not work for another. It's about finding the right balance for your content and audience. This means continuously testing new strategies, analyzing the results, and being ready to pivot your approach based on what you learn.

Finally, patience and persistence are your best friends on this journey. Changes you make today might not yield immediate results, but they lay the groundwork for future success. Success on YouTube is a long-term game, and those willing to stay the course, adapt to changes, and continually strive to understand and leverage the algorithm will come out on top.

In this rapidly changing digital landscape, your ability to adapt is your greatest asset. Stay curious, stay flexible, and remember that each change in the YouTube algorithm is not a hurdle but an opportunity to learn, grow, and ultimately, succeed.

As you continue to navigate through the complexities of YouTube's algorithm, keep your focus on creating valuable, engaging content for your audience. This is what truly matters at the end of the day. Your adaptability, combined with a commitment to your audience, will ensure your faceless channel not only survives but thrives amidst the algorithm's ebbs and flows.

Experimenting with New Content Formats

Staying ahead of the curve in the dynamic landscape of YouTube demands not just creativity but also a willingness to experiment and innovate. In the realm of faceless YouTube channels, this is even more crucial, given the unique challenges and advantages these channels present. Trying out new content formats is not just an option; it's a necessity for those aiming to carve out a significant presence on the platform.

Let's dive deeper into why experimenting with new content formats can be a game-changer. First, it helps you stand out. The digital space is cluttered with creators doing similar things. By bringing something new to the table, you capture the curiosity and interest of viewers. This doesn't mean reinventing the wheel but perhaps offering a new spin on existing concepts.

Consider the evolution of video content formats on YouTube. From standard vlogs to 360-degree videos, creators who leap and adapt to new formats often find themselves ahead of the pack. As a faceless channel, exploring formats like animated explainers, motion graphics, or interactive videos could set you apart and open up new audience segments.

Engagement is another critical factor. Experimenting with content formats can lead to more engaging videos that keep viewers hooked and coming back for more. Interactive content, for example, offers viewers a say in the narrative or outcome of the video, making the viewing experience more personal and memorable.

Moreover, trying new formats can lead to unexpected discoveries about your audience. You might find that your viewers prefer a particular type of content that you hadn't considered before. This insight can be invaluable for refining your content strategy and tailoring your offerings to match audience preferences more closely.

But how do you start experimenting with new content formats? First, keep an eye on emerging trends both within and outside your niche. What's gaining traction? Can it be adapted to a faceless channel format? Next, evaluate the feasibility. Consider your resources, skills, and the potential need for new tools or software.

Don't forget the power of pilot tests. Before fully committing to a new format, create a pilot episode or a mini-series. Analyze viewer feedback, engagement metrics, and the overall performance of these tests to make informed decisions on whether or not to fully adopt the new format.

Collaboration can also spark innovation. Partnering with other creators, particularly those in slightly different niches or those who are pioneering new formats, can provide fresh ideas and insights. This can help you blend different elements to create something truly unique for your channel.

Feedback loops are, however, the cornerstone of successful experimentation. Engaging with your audience, requesting their input, and incorporating their feedback not only improves content quality but also builds a stronger community around your channel. Your viewers feel valued and part of your creative journey, fostering loyalty and enhancing retention.

Technical proficiency should not be overlooked either. Learning new software, tools, or techniques is often part of experimenting with new content formats. While this can be challenging, it's also an opportunity to enhance your skills and improve your channel's production value.

Risks are inherent in experimentation, but so are the rewards. Some attempts might not pan out as expected, but failure is an integral part of the learning process. These experiences can provide valuable lessons and insights that guide future content strategies.

To mitigate risks, it's wise to start small and gradually increase the scale of your experiments. This incremental approach allows you to manage resources effectively while testing the waters with new ideas. It also reduces the impact of any single failed experiment.

Finally, document your journey. Share your experimentation processes, successes, and failures with your audience. This transparency not only humanizes your channel but also can inspire and educate other creators. It positions you as a thought leader in the faceless YouTube channel space, attracting more viewers and potential collaborations.

In conclusion, embracing experimentation with new content formats is essential for staying ahead in the constantly evolving world of YouTube. It requires curiosity, a willingness to learn and adapt, and an understanding that success is often found just outside your comfort zone. By being innovative and forward-thinking, you can ensure that your faceless YouTube channel not only survives but thrives in this competitive landscape.

Remember, the goal isn't simply to follow trends but to set them. By experimenting with new content formats, you're not just adapting to the present—you're shaping the future of your channel and potentially influencing the direction of content creation on YouTube at large.

Harnessing the Power of YouTube Shorts

The digital landscape is ever-evolving, and one of the most dynamic shifts we've seen in recent years is the rise of short-form content. YouTube Shorts has emerged as a key player in this revolution, offering a platform for creators to share snippets that are quick, engaging, and capable of capturing the fleeting attention spans of today's audience. As part of our journey to stay ahead of the curve, let's dive deep into how you can leverage YouTube Shorts to propel your faceless channel forward.

First things first, YouTube Shorts are not just traditional videos cut into shorter segments; they're a breed of their own. Think of them as your elevator pitch to potential subscribers. Each Short offers a chance to showcase the essence of your content in 60 seconds or less. This format's beauty lies in its brevity and the opportunity it presents for creativity and virality. Imagine getting your message across, sparking interest, and driving engagement, all within a minute's worth of content.

To begin with, understanding the algorithm of YouTube Shorts is pivotal. Just like with longer content, the algorithm favors videos that keep viewers hooked and coming back for more. However, the game-changer here is 'the loop effect.' A Short that encourages multiple views not only boosts its own visibility but can also serve as a gateway to your longer content. It's about creating that irresistible hook that viewers can't just watch once.

When crafting your Shorts, think visually stimulating and audibly engaging. Since the goal is to hold attention from start to finish, every second counts. Use vibrant visuals, enticing thumbnails, and catchy audio to grab attention. Remember, in the fast-paced world of Shorts, your content needs to stand out in the blink of an eye.

Let's talk strategy. Incorporating YouTube Shorts into your content calendar should not be an afterthought but a well-integrated part of your content ecosystem. Plan your Shorts with intention, using them to complement your longer videos. This could mean creating teaser content for an upcoming video, providing quick tips related to your niche, or even sharing behind-the-scenes glimpses.

One of the most compelling aspects of YouTube Shorts is its accessibility. You don't need high-end equipment or extensive video editing skills. Most successful Shorts are shot on smartphones and edited with basic editing tools. This ease of content creation lowers the barrier to entry, making it an excellent starting point for new creators or a fun, low-pressure addition for seasoned YouTubers.

Engagement doesn't end at just creating and posting your Short. Interacting with your audience through comments, challenges, and calls-to-action within your Shorts can foster a sense of community and belonging. Engage viewers by asking questions, encouraging them to share their thoughts, or even create response Shorts. This two-way interaction can significantly boost your channel's engagement metrics.

Don't just stop at posting your Shorts on YouTube. Maximizing their reach means sharing them across your other social platforms. Instagram Stories, Twitter, and Facebook pages are great places to cross-promote your content. By doing so, you're not only boosting your Shorts' exposure but also directing traffic back to your YouTube channel.

Analytics play a critical role in shaping your Shorts strategy. Regularly check your Shorts' performance metrics to understand what's resonating with your audience. Look for patterns in view counts, likes, shares, and comments to inform your future content creation. This data-driven approach ensures that you're not just creating content in the dark but are aligned with your audience's preferences.

Collaboration can significantly amplify your Shorts' reach. Partnering with other creators for challenges or duets can expose your content to new audiences. Such collaborations not only increase your visibility but also offer fresh content ideas and creative perspectives, keeping your feed vibrant and engaging.

SEO isn't just for long-form videos. Optimizing your Shorts with relevant keywords, hashtags, and catchy titles makes them more discoverable. Treat the description and title of your Short as if you're optimizing a full-length video. By injecting your Shorts with searchable terms, you're effectively increasing your visibility in YouTube searches and the Shorts shelf.

Experimentation is key. The beauty of YouTube Shorts lies in its versatility and the freedom it provides creators to test different content types without the commitment of long-form content. Use this to your advantage by experimenting with various formats, styles, and content types to see what resonates best with your audience.

Incorporating YouTube Shorts into your monetization strategy can be a game-changer. While the path to monetization may differ from traditional videos, the engagement and audience growth driven by Shorts can lead to increased views on your monetized content, affiliate clicks, and even merchandise sales. View Shorts not just as standalone content but as a valuable piece of your larger channel monetization puzzle.

Remember, the goal is to add value to your audience, regardless of the content's length. Shorts offer a unique way to connect with viewers, share insights, and entertain, all while driving traffic to your channel. It's about striking the right balance between entertaining quick-hits and the in-depth content that establishes you as an authority in your niche.

Finally, staying ahead of the curve means continuously evolving with the platform. As you delve into the world of YouTube Shorts, keep an ear to the ground for updates, new features, and best practices. The digital landscape is fast-paced, but with YouTube Shorts, you've got a powerful tool at your fingertips to keep your content fresh, engaging, and ahead of the curve.

As we wrap up this section, remember that YouTube Shorts are more than just a trend; they're a potent tool for growth, engagement, and creativity. By strategically incorporating Shorts into your content repertoire, you're not only broadening your channel's appeal but also setting the stage for lasting success. So go ahead, capture the moment, tell a story, and let your Shorts propel your channel to new heights.

Future Trends and Opportunities

In a digital landscape as vast and ever-evolving as YouTube, staying ahead of the curve isn't just advantageous; it's imperative for anyone looking to carve out a niche and generate passive income through faceless channels. As we delve into the future trends and opportunities that await, remember that each trend represents not just a challenge, but a doorway to untold possibilities for growth, engagement, and monetization.

The integration of artificial intelligence and machine learning within YouTube's algorithms is something creators can't afford to ignore. This technology is not only reshaping how content is discovered but also how it's created. Creators who leverage AI for content ideas, video editing, and even generating voiceovers will find themselves at a significant advantage. The key is to use these tools not as a replacement for human creativity but as a complement to enhance productivity and creativity.

Virtual Reality (VR) and Augmented Reality (AR) are set to redefine the viewer experience on YouTube. As hardware becomes more accessible, faceless channels that start experimenting with immersive content today will stand out tomorrow. Whether it's through 360-degree videos or interactive experiences, the potential for creators to transport their audience into their content is boundless.

Another burgeoning trend is the rise of niche and hyper-niche channels. The broader your topic, the more competition you face. However, diving deep into specific interests not only reduces competition but also fosters a highly engaged community. This specificity can significantly enhance your channel's discoverability and appeal to both viewers and advertisers.

With the explosion of short-form content, exemplified by YouTube Shorts, creators have a chance to capture the ever-decreasing attention spans of viewers. But it's not just about creating shorter content; it's about mastering the art of storytelling in bite-sized pieces. Engaging viewers within the first few seconds and offering unique, easily consumable content could catapult a faceless channel into viral fame.

Likewise, live streaming continues to gain traction, offering real-time engagement that other formats can't match. For faceless channels, this could mean live-streaming events, behind-the-scenes looks, or even interactive sessions using animated characters or avatars. The authenticity and immediacy of live content can significantly boost audience loyalty.

The integration of e-commerce on YouTube is also an area ripe with opportunities. With features like product tags and in-video shopping, creators can transform their content into a direct sales channel. This is especially lucrative for channels that focus on reviews, tutorials, and any content where products are featured or discussed.

As we look to the future, cross-platform promotion will become even more critical. Your YouTube channel shouldn't exist in isolation. Harnessing the power of social media platforms, newsletters, and blogs to drive traffic to your YouTube content can amplify your reach and, in turn, your revenue.

User-generated content and community collaborations will also take center stage. Empowering your audience to contribute ideas or even content can foster a sense of community and belonging, crucial for building a loyal subscriber base. Plus, collaborations with other creators or brands can open up your channel to new audiences.

Never underestimate the power of data analytics. Understanding your audience's behavior, preferences, and engagement patterns can help you tailor your content strategy to meet their needs. YouTube's analytics tools are incredibly powerful, and creators who dive deep into this data will have a significant edge.

Sustainability and social responsibility will become increasingly important themes on YouTube. Audiences are more conscious of the environmental and ethical implications of the content they consume. Channels that embody these values or actively contribute to positive change can resonate more deeply with viewers.

Finally, consider the global nature of YouTube. Creating content that transcends cultural and linguistic barriers can open your channel to international markets. Whether it's through subtitled videos, universal themes, or content specifically tailored to non-English speaking audiences, the global stage is vast and varied.

Embarking on the journey to capitalize on these future trends and opportunities requires a blend of creativity, adaptability, and forward-thinking. As you push the boundaries of what's possible with your faceless YouTube channel, remember that the essence of success lies not just in following trends but in anticipating them. It's about seeing the unseen, hearing the unspoken, and creating content that speaks to the future.

So, as you look ahead, let these opportunities inspire you, challenge you, and propel you toward your goal of building a thriving, income-generating faceless YouTube channel. The future is bright, and the digital landscape is yours to shape.

The journey of a thousand miles begins with a single step. And for you, that step is recognizing the boundless opportunities that lie ahead. Embrace them, explore them, and let them guide you as you continue to carve your path in the vast expanse of YouTube.

Chapter 11

Case Studies and Success Stories

By now, you've got the nuts and bolts of starting a faceless YouTube channel, right from finding your niche to setting up monetization streams. But let's be real, nothing beats seeing these strategies in live action. In this chapter, we dive into some heart-pumping, inspiring success stories from creators who've been in your shoes. They started with an idea—maybe a bit fuzzy at first—and turned it into a thriving faceless YouTube channel. We're not just talking about big numbers here, but the journey: the setbacks, the eureka moments, and the relentless pursuit of improvement. Each case study is a treasure trove of lessons, showing you what worked wonders and what flopped hard. It's like having a roadmap where the potholes are clearly marked, so you know exactly where to tread carefully. Plus, we'll share priceless insights from industry experts who've seen it all. They'll let you in on the common pitfalls most new creators fall into and arm you with strategies to dodge them like a pro or bounce back if you do stumble. Think of this chapter as your dose of motivation mixed with hard-won wisdom, showing you that the path to success on YouTube is as diverse as the creators who walk it. So, whether you're envisioning your channel as a side hustle or your full-time gig, these success stories are here to light that fire within you and keep it blazing.

Deep Dives into Successful Faceless Channels

Imagine launching a YouTube channel without ever showing your face, yet still raking in views and revenue that outpace some traditional vloggers. Sounds intriguing, right? That's the hallmark of faceless YouTube channels, a trend that's been transforming how we approach content creation. In this section, we'll explore the magic behind some of the most successful faceless channels, uncovering strategies and insights that you can apply to your own journey.

Let's start with the basics. A faceless YouTube channel focuses on content that doesn't require on-camera talent. From animation and commentary to compilations and tutorials, these channels leverage creativity and resourcefulness, proving that personality isn't just tied to a face. It's tied to the content's voice and value.

One standout example is a channel that dives into mysterious historical events without ever revealing who's behind the narration. The channel has mastered the art of storytelling, using suspenseful scripts and engaging visuals. The key takeaway? A strong narrative can captivate an audience regardless of the narrator's anonymity.

Another success story comes from a channel specializing in meditation and sleep music. Here, the creator taps into the power of SEO, optimizing video titles, descriptions, and tags that rank high for relaxation-related searches. This strategy underscores the importance of understanding your audience's search intent and optimizing your content to meet their needs.

Let's not overlook channels that curate and comment on viral video content. By adding insightful or humorous commentary to trending videos, these creators provide added value, keeping viewers entertained and engaged. This approach highlights the potential of piggybacking on existing trends while adding your unique spin.

Animation channels also represent a significant segment of successful faceless channels. These creators use compelling characters and storylines to discuss current events, educate, or simply entertain. The brilliance here lies in the combination of high-quality animation and timely, relevant content, demonstrating that visual storytelling can be incredibly powerful without an on-screen presence.

How-to and tutorial channels thrive as faceless entities by delivering clear, conciseinformation on a wide range of topics. Whether it's tech tips, cooking recipes, or DIY projects, these channels focus on providing value above all else. They prove that expertise and the ability to explain complex topics in simple terms can garner a loyal following.

A unique niche that's emerged within the faceless channel space is that of ambient sound creators. Channels that feature hours of natural soundscapes or city noises offer a form of escape for listeners, highlighting the broad range of content types that can succeed without a personal brand front and center.

Gaming channels, particularly those focusing on let's plays, walkthroughs, and strategy guides, have long embraced the faceless model. These creators let their gameplay do the talking, often complemented by voiceover commentary. They leverage the huge appetite for gaming content, proving you don't need to be on camera to be a part of the gaming community.

Compilations channels take advantage of the wealth of content available across the internet, curating clips around specific themes or interests. The creativity here lies in the selection, sequencing, and presentation of these clips to create a new viewing experience. It shows how curation can be as creative an endeavor as original content creation.

Storytime and narration channels that feature animated or static visuals while a narrator tells a story have capitalized on the human love for storytelling. These channels focus on the quality of the narrative and the skill of the narrator to evoke emotions, proving the age-old power of a good story.

In the realm of educational content, channels that simplify complex subjects like science, math, or history have garnered millions of followers. These creators use animations, diagrams, and voiceovers to make learning accessible and entertaining. Their success underlines the demand for content that enriches as it entertains.

Looking at these examples, several common themes emerge. First is the focus on delivering high-quality content that meets a specific need or solves a specific problem. Secondly, successful faceless channels understand and leverage SEO to ensure their content gets seen. Third, they often tap into trends or niches with a dedicated audience looking for that type of content.

What's particularly exciting about these channels is the diversity of content and approaches they represent. It's a testament to the limitless possibilities of YouTube as a platform for creators who may not want to be in the limelight but still have valuable content to share.

In conclusion, building a successful faceless YouTube channel hinges on understanding your audience, delivering consistently high-quality content, and optimizing for discoverability. It requires creativity, strategy, and a bit of courage to go against the grain. But as these case studies show, the rewards can be substantial. Whether you're a budding creator or looking to pivot your strategy, let these success stories inspire you to explore the potential of faceless channels. Who knows? Your channel could be the next big hit without you ever having to show your face.

Armed with these insights, you're better equipped to carve out your niche in the expansive world of YouTube. Remember, success doesn't come overnight, but with persistence, innovation, and a focus on quality, your faceless channel can achieve remarkable success.

Lessons Learned from Industry Experts

Delving into the universe of faceless YouTube channels can feel like navigating a jungle. The paths to success are many, but so are the pitfalls. Fortunately, industry experts have blazed trails we can follow, sharing nuggets of wisdom that hinge on practicality, creativity, and strategic insight. Here, we'll explore these lessons, transforming their experiences into a guidebook for your journey.

One pivotal lesson comes from understanding your audience's wants and desires. Success isn't just about creating content; it's about creating the right content. Experts emphasize the importance of tuning into your target demographic, understanding their challenges, and tailoring your content to address those needs directly.

Consistency is another cornerstone of success. This isn't just about sticking to a posting schedule, although that's important. It's about maintaining a consistent theme, quality, and voice across your videos. This consistency helps in building a brand that viewers can recognize and trust.

Optimization for search engines, or SEO, is a skill set that can't be overlooked. The internet's most successful faceless channels know how to make their content discoverable. This involves a deep dive into keyword research, crafting compelling titles and descriptions, and leveraging tags and hashtags. YouTube is a search engine as much as it is a social platform, and treating it as such can dramatically increase your channel's visibility.

Another key takeaway is the power of collaboration. Teaming up with creators who share your audience but not your content can introduce your channel to viewers who are likely to be interested in your videos. Collaboration is a two-way street that offers mutual benefits through shared audiences.

Effective storytelling is also at the heart of engaging content. It's not just what you communicate but how you do it. The ability to weave information into a compelling narrative can significantly enhance viewer retention and engagement. It's storytelling that turns viewers into subscribers, and subscribers into a community.

Speaking of community, never underestimate its power. Successful faceless channels engage with their viewers through comments, polls, and social media platforms. This engagement fosters a sense of belonging among your audience, transforming passive viewers into active participants in your channel's journey.

Diversification of revenue is another lesson that cannot be overstated. Relying solely on ad revenue is risky. The experts suggest exploring affiliate marketing, sponsorships, and even the sale of digital products or merchandise. This diversification can provide financial stability to your channel, ensuring its longevity.

Learning to adapt is crucial in the ever-evolving landscape of YouTube. What works today may not work tomorrow. The top players in the industry stay ahead by keeping an eye on trends, algorithm changes, and new features, continuously experimenting and evolving their strategies accordingly.

Investing back into your channel is a practice championed by many successful creators. Whether it's upgrading equipment, investing in advertising, or hiring help for editing, allocating resources back into your channel can spur growth and improve the quality of your content.

Understanding the technical side of content creation, such as editing software, audio quality, and thumbnail design, significantly affects your channel's professional appearance. Learning these skills or collaborating with professionals who have them can make your content stand out.

Building an email list or a community outside of YouTube is a strategy often overlooked but highly effective. It serves as insurance against algorithm changes or shifts in platform policies and provides a direct line of communication with your most dedicated followers.

Patience and perseverance emerge as perhaps the most universal lessons. Success rarely happens overnight. It's the result of consistent effort, learning from failures, and the tenacity to keep going despite setbacks.

Finally, never stop learning. The top creators are perpetual students. They read extensively, attend workshops, and are always on the lookout for new strategies to adopt. This mindset of growth not only keeps their content fresh but also keeps them motivated and inspired.

Each of these lessons, forged in the fires of experience, offers a beacon for aspiring creators. Implementing these strategies won't guarantee success overnight, but they provide a solid foundation upon which to build a sustainable faceless YouTube channel. Let these insights inspire you, guide you, and most importantly, remind you that the path to success is a journey of learning, adapting, and persevering.

Common Pitfalls to Avoid and How to Overcome Them

When diving into the world of faceless YouTube channels, you're bound to face some hurdles. But fear not! Let's break down these common pitfalls and how you can gracefully leap over them to achieve success.

First and foremost, a classic trap many fall into is underestimating the importance of niche selection. It's easy to jump into a niche because it seems lucrative, but if there's no passion or knowledge to back it up, the content will suffer. The key here? Dive deep into your interests and expertise areas. If you're genuinely interested in what you're creating, it'll resonate more with your audience, and the process will be much more enjoyable for you.

Another pitfall is neglecting video quality. We get it, you might not have a blockbuster budget, but that doesn't mean your videos can't look professional. Many creators skip investing time in learning basic video editing skills or using quality graphics, which can drastically impact the viewer's experience. Overcoming this means dedicating time to learn and utilize available tools and resources that can enhance your video quality without breaking the bank.

Ignoring SEO is like hiding your content under a rock. If you're not optimizing your videos for search, you're missing out on a massive opportunity for visibility. Use relevant keywords in your titles, descriptions, and tags to ensure your videos are discoverable. Remember, YouTube is a search engine too, and a well-optimized video can lead to exponential growth.

Engagement is another area where many creators stumble. It's not just about posting videos and waiting for views to roll in. Engage with your audience through comments, polls, and social media. Creating a community around your channel not only boosts your channel's loyalty but also makes your journey a lot more fulfilling.

Consistency issues plague even the best creators. Starting a channel with a flurry of videos and then disappearing for months is a common narrative. Consistency doesn't mean posting every day; it means setting a realistic schedule and sticking to it, whether it's once a week or twice a month. This helps build a loyal viewership that knows when to expect your content.

Chasing viral trends can be tempting, but it's a slippery slope. While it's essential to stay relevant, completely altering your content to jump on every trend can alienate your audience. Stay true to your channel's mission and sprinkle in trends in a way that complements your content strategy.

Monetization missteps are all too common. Many creators either monetize too early, which can turn off viewers, or too late, missing out on potential revenue. Strike a balance by focusing on growing your audience first and then exploring monetization methods that align with your content and audience preferences.

Neglecting analytics is akin to flying blind. YouTube provides a wealth of data that can inform your content strategy. Not analyzing this data means you're missing out on insights about what's working and what isn't. Regularly review your analytics to refine your approach and boost your channel's performance.

Isolation can be a creator's downfall. Collaborating with other creators can open up your channel to new audiences and bring fresh perspectives to your content. Network within your niche to find collaboration opportunities that benefit all parties involved.

Lastly, many creators get discouraged by slow growth and give up too soon. Success on YouTube is rarely overnight. It requires patience, persistence, and a willingness to adapt and learn. If you're passionate about your content and committed to delivering value to your viewers, growth will come.

To wrap it up, jumping into the world of faceless YouTube channels is an exciting adventure, but like any journey, it's filled with its share of obstacles. However, with the right mindset, strategies, and a pinch of creativity, these pitfalls can not only be avoided but turned into stepping stones for success. So keep creating, keep learning, and remember – every great channel started with a single video.

Embracing these solutions to common pitfalls not only smoothens your path to YouTube success but also enhances your growth journey. It's about making informed decisions, learning from your setbacks, and continuously striving to deliver value to your audience. With perseverance, adaptability, and a focus on quality, your faceless

YouTube channel can transform into a source of inspiration, entertainment, and, yes, passive income.

Remember, your channel's success is not just measured by the number of subscribers or views but by the impact you make on your audience and the fulfillment you derive from your creative journey. So go ahead, steer clear of these pitfalls, and carve your path to becoming a cherished creator in the bustling world of YouTube.

Conclusion

We started this journey together with a clear goal in mind: to empower you with the knowledge and strategies necessary to build and master your faceless YouTube channel, and in doing so, create a stream of passive income that can sustain and grow with time. From finding your niche to creating content that resonates, from understanding SEO to engage your audience, and finally, to monetize and create passive income streams, we've covered a vast terrain. Now, you stand at a pivotal point, equipped with the insights and tools needed to carve out your success in the digital world.

The path to building a sustainable faceless YouTube channel is both exhilarating and challenging, but remember, your journey doesn't end here. It's continuous, filled with learning and adapting. You have the foundation, but the digital landscape is always evolving, and your ability to stay ahead lies in your commitment to innovation and growth. So, take the next steps with confidence, keep experimenting, and remember the power of persistence. Your passion coupled with the strategies outlined in these pages is a recipe for success. Here's to creating, scaling, and thriving in your faceless YouTube venture!

Recap of Key Insights and Strategies

What a journey it's been! From exploring the ins and outs of creating a faceless YouTube channel to uncovering the strategies that can turn these platforms into significant income streams, we've covered a lot. Now, let's take a moment to recap some of the most vital insights and strategies that can help you transform your creative endeavors into success.

First, understanding your niche is non-negotiable. We dug into the importance of identifying your passion and expertise while aligning it with market demand. Remember, the key is to find that sweet spot where your interests meet what viewers are seeking. This doesn't just ensure content authenticity but also increases your channel's potential to resonate with a larger audience.

Strategy formulation has been another critical area we've emphasized. Setting clear, actionable goals and mapping out your content in a structured calendar paves the way for consistency. Consistency, as we learned, isn't just about posting regularly; it's about maintaining quality, staying true to your channel's voice, and delivering value to your audience.

On setting up your channel, we highlighted the significance of those first impressions. A memorable channel name, engaging banner, and compelling description contribute to a strong foundation. They don't just attract viewers; they start building your brand from the moment someone lays eyes on your channel page.

Content is king, but engagement is queen. Our discussions around storytelling techniques, voiceover tips, and utilizing royalty-free media were about crafting content that hooks viewers from the first second. Moreover, optimizing videos for SEO through researched keywords, eye-catching thumbnails, and clever titles is what makes your videos discoverable.

Uploading and publishing videos isn't just a final step; it's a strategic one. We explored the perfect upload routine, including timing and frequency, incorporating effective end screens, and why subtitles or captions can be a game-changer in reaching broader audiences.

Growing and engaging with your audience means embracing social media, engaging in the comments, and collaborating with other creators. Every interaction is an opportunity to enhance your community and brand loyalty, which is invaluable for long-term growth.

When it comes to monetization, diversity is your best friend. We delved into multiple revenue streams from ad revenue and affiliate marketing to selling digital products. Balancing these can not only increase your income but also cushion against changes in any single revenue source.

The concept of creating passive income streams has been a recurring theme, emphasizing the power of automation and scaling. Whether through content syndication, digital products, or expanding into multiple channels, the goal is to build income sources that grow even when not actively working on them.

Staying ahead of the curve is all about adaptation and innovation. We covered the significance of keeping up with YouTube algorithm changes, experimenting with content formats, and capitalizing on trends like YouTube Shorts to keep your channel dynamic and engaging.

Learning from successful faceless channels provided us with concrete examples and actionable insights. It's one thing to discuss strategies in theory; it's another to see how they're executed in real life. Each case study was a lesson in creativity, perseverance, and strategic planning.

On avoiding common pitfalls, we noted the importance of not stretching yourself too thin, avoiding content that doesn't align with your brand, and the dangers of neglecting audience engagement. Overcoming these hurdles is about learning, adjusting, and persisting.

And let's not forget about the vast amount of tools and resources available. From editing software to keyword research tools, leveraging these can significantly enhance your productivity and content quality. It's about working smarter, not just harder.

As you move forward, remember, building a successful faceless YouTube channel is a journey filled with learning and growth. It requires patience, creativity, and resilience. But with the strategies and insights shared, you're now equipped to carve out your niche, engage an audience, and build a revenue-generating channel that lasts.

So, take these strategies, apply them with your unique twist, and embark on your journey to success. The road might be challenging, but the potential rewards, financial freedom, and creative satisfaction are truly worth the effort. Let's get creating!

Your Next Steps Toward Success

Now that we've journeyed through the ins and outs of building a faceless YouTube channel that stands out, the ball is firmly in your court. It's one thing to absorb information, but the real magic happens when you put that knowledge into action. So, let's walk through your next steps toward creating a channel that not only exists but thrives and becomes a source of passive income for you.

First things first, let's recap on the importance of niching down. You've heard it already: a jack of all trades is a master of none. This is particularly true on YouTube. Your first action item is to zero in on a niche that you're passionate about and that has an audience. Remember, passion intersects with profitability when you solve a specific problem or entertain a specific group of people in a way that no one else does.

Next, craft your strategy. This isn't as daunting as it sounds. Start with setting some clear, achievable goals. What does success look like for you in three months, six months, a year? Break these down into smaller, actionable steps, such as creating your first ten videos or reaching your first thousand subscribers. A goal without a plan is just a wish, so solidify your strategy.

Setting up your channel properly cannot be overlooked. Choose a channel name and design that reflects your niche and grabs attention. Your channel banner and logo are the first things potential subscribers see, so make them count. Similarly, spend time crafting a compelling channel description that clearly explains why viewers should stick around.

Content creation is where you get to flex your creative muscles. Use storytelling techniques to make your videos more engaging and memorable. Invest time in scripting, finding the right voiceover talent, and selecting royalty-free media that enhances your narrative. Editing is where your video comes to life, so familiarize yourself with some tools and software that can help streamline this process.

Don't forget about SEO. YouTube is the second largest search engine in the world, and if you're not optimizing your videos for search, you're missing out on a massive opportunity. Conduct keyword research to understand what your potential viewers are looking for, and craft your titles, descriptions, and thumbnails to match. Be strategic about tags and hashtags to broaden your video's reach.

Uploading and publishing your videos is more than just hitting "Publish." Timing can significantly affect your video's initial performance. Learn the best times to post based on your target audience's viewing habits, and stick to a consistent schedule to keep your audience engaged.

Growth and engagement are interlinked on YouTube. Engage with your community through comments, polls, and social media. Collaboration with other creators can also introduce your channel to new audiences. Keep an eye on your analytics to understand what works and what doesn't, and adapt accordingly.

Monetization should be approached with a plan. Beyond joining the YouTube Partner Program, explore diverse revenue streams such as affiliate marketing, sponsorships, and selling your digital products or merchandise. Passive income won't happen overnight, but with the right strategies, it can become a significant part of your earnings.

Create passive income streams by automating and scaling your operations where possible. Invest in tools or outsource certain tasks to focus on content creation and strategy. Exploring licensing and syndicating your content can also open up new revenue channels.

Staying ahead of the curve involves constant learning and adaptation. The digital landscape, especially YouTube, is always evolving. Keep experimenting with new content formats, stay updated with trends, and never be afraid to pivot your strategy if something isn't working.

Remember, success on YouTube, particularly with a faceless channel, doesn't happen by chance. It's the result of consistent effort, strategic planning, and the willingness to learn from mistakes. Embrace the journey, celebrate your milestones, no matter how small, and always seek to provide value to your audience.

Finally, remember why you started. It's easy to get caught up in the numbers game - views, likes, subscribers. Yet, the core of your channel should always be your passion for the content you create and the value you provide to your viewers. Stay true to that, and success will follow.

Your next steps are clear. It's time to move from planning to action. Start today. Take that first step, no matter how small it may seem. Every big achievement begins with the decision to try. Go out there, create, engage, and let your faceless YouTube channel be the start of something incredible.

Remember, the only way to fail is not to start. So, take a deep breath, focus on your goals, and take that first step towards creating a successful, income-generating faceless YouTube channel. Your future self will thank you for the courage to begin today.

Building a Sustainable Faceless YouTube Channel

As we approach the conclusion of our journey, it's essential to focus on the cornerstone of long-term success: building a sustainable faceless YouTube channel. Sustainability isn't just about keeping your channel alive; it's about fostering an environment where growth, innovation, and engagement are part of your daily routine. Let's dive into how you can build a channel that stands the test of time, even when your face isn't the front of the show.

Firstly, sustainability in the YouTube space begins with understanding your content deeply. It's about knowing what resonates with your audience and delivering it consistently. This doesn't mean you can't explore new ideas or content formats. On the contrary, innovation keeps your channel vibrant and exciting. However, having a solid grasp on the core themes and values that define your channel ensures that your explorations remain grounded and relevant to your audience.

Secondly, creating a sustainable channel is closely tied to developing efficient workflows. Whether you're managing the channel solo or with a team, setting up systems that streamline production, from research and scripting to editing and publishing, will save you time and stress. This efficiency not only boosts your channel's output but also safeguards your creative spark from burning out.

Investing in evergreen content is another crucial strategy. While trending topics can give you a temporary boost in views, evergreen content remains relevant, continuing to attract viewers long after it's published. This type of content becomes the bedrock of your channel, providing a stable viewership base that can be crucial during slower growth periods.

Moreover, understanding analytics goes beyond checking how many views or subscribers you've gained. It's about diving deep into audience behavior, understanding watch times, drop-off points, and what content drives engagement. These insights allow you to refine your content strategy continuously, ensuring that your channel evolves in alignment with your audience's preferences.

Furthermore, leveraging social media platforms to bolster your YouTube channel can't be overlooked. Even without showing your face, there are numerous creative ways to promote your content across social media, from sneak peeks and highlights to engaging directly with your audience. This multi-platform presence expands your reach, drawing in viewers from various corners of the internet.

Community building is another aspect that sustains your channel over the long haul. Interacting with your viewers through comments, polls, or Q&A sessions fosters a sense of belonging and investment in your channel's success. This loyal community becomes a powerful asset, promoting your content organically and providing supportive feedback.

Financial sustainability is, of course, a major concern. Diversifying your income streams through methods like affiliate marketing, merchandise, or even creating your own digital products can help buffer against fluctuations in ad revenue. This financial stability allows you more creative freedom and the ability to invest back into your channel for quality improvements.

In terms of content, diversification is equally important. While maintaining a clear niche is crucial for brand identity, subtly exploring related areas or content types can attract new viewers and keep your current audience engaged. This strategy prevents your channel from becoming stagnant and keeps the content fresh and exciting.

Adapting to changes in the YouTube algorithm requires flexibility and a willingness to evolve. Staying informed about platform updates and modifying your content strategy accordingly is essential for maintaining visibility and growth. This might mean adjusting your video length, experimenting with new content formats, or enhancing your video's SEO.

Speaking of SEO, continually optimizing your videos for search remains a cornerstone of sustainable growth. This involves keeping abreast of the best practices for titles, descriptions, and keywords, ensuring that your content continues to reach its intended audience amid YouTube's ever-changing landscape.

Collaborations with other creators can inject new life into your channel, introducing your content to new audiences while providing fresh perspectives to your existing viewers. This mutually beneficial strategy can lead to long-term partnerships and community building within the creator ecosystem.

Creative storytelling and high-quality video production are non-negotiable for a channel's long-term success. Investing time and resources into improving your storytelling techniques and production quality sets your channel apart in a crowded marketplace. It's a testament to your commitment to excellence and respect for your audience.

Lastly, staying true to your passion and why you started your channel is vital. This intrinsic motivation is what keeps you going through the ups and downs of the YouTube journey. Remembering your core mission and audience needs helps maintain your focus and drive, ensuring that your channel continues to grow and inspire.

As we wrap up, remember that sustainability is not just a destination; it's a continuous process of learning, adapting, and growing. Your faceless YouTube channel can achieve enduring success through dedication, creativity, and a deep connection with your audience. So here's to your success, to the resilience of your channel, and to the remarkable journey ahead. Keep pushing boundaries, stay curious, and never underestimate the impact of your content.

Appendix A: Appendix

If you've made it this far, hats off to you. You're not just dreaming about making a splash in the world of faceless YouTube channels; you're on the verge of actually doing it. This appendix isn't just a collection of add-ons. Think of it as your treasure chest, the ace up your sleeve, ensuring you're not left adrift in the vast YouTube ocean.

Sample Channel Templates and Scripts

Ever stared at a blank screen, wondering how to start your video script? Or maybe puzzled over how your channel's homepage should look? You're not alone. Even the most creative minds hit a wall sometimes. But here's a little secret – using templates doesn't mean sacrificing originality. It means giving your creativity a structure to flourish in. Inside, you'll find customizable templates and script outlines tailored for various types of content. From how-to videos to listicles, these templates are designed to kickstart your creativity and help you produce compelling content that resonates with your audience.

Checklists for Starting and Growing Your Channel

Keeping track of everything you need to do to launch and grow your channel can feel like juggling flaming torches. Miss one, and the whole show could go up in smoke. But fear not. Included here are comprehensive checklists that cover everything from channel setup essentials to post-launch promotion strategies. These aren's just any checklists; they're your roadmap to success. They ensure you dot every i and cross every t, from optimizing your channel description to scheduling your content calendar. Following these checklists will not only make the process smoother but will also set you up for long-term growth.

In wrapping up, remember this journey you're embarking on is uniquely yours. Tools, templates, and checklists are here to guide you, but your creativity and passion are what will truly set your channel apart. Stay focused, stay inspired, and let's make your faceless channel not just a source of income, but a source of pride.

Good luck, and here's to creating something incredible.

Sample Channel Templates and Scripts

Embarking on your YouTube journey, especially if you've decided to run a faceless channel, might seem like navigating through a dense jungle. But, fear not! In this section, we're going to provide you with some solid templates and script ideas that serve as your compass. These are designed to help you create content that captures attention, engages your audience, and, most importantly, drives your passive income goals.

First off, let's talk about why templates and scripts are your best friends. They not only streamline your content creation process but also ensure consistency—a critical factor in building a loyal viewer base. Think of your favorite TV show and how its structure keeps you coming back. That's the power of a good template.

Variety, however, is the spice of life. While we advocate for consistency, injecting different content formats within your chosen niche can keep things interesting. For instance, if your channel focuses on mindfulness and meditation, your content could range from guided meditation sessions to informative pieces on the benefits of mindfulness.

Bearing that in mind, let's dive into a sample script structure that can be adapted across various niches:

1. **Introduction:** Start with a catchy opener that clearly states what the viewer will gain by watching your video. It should be compelling enough to make them stay.
2. **Problem Statement:** Identify a common problem or question your target audience has. This establishes a connection and sets the stage for the solution you're about to provide.
3. **Solution Overview:** Offer a brief overview of the solution you're going to delve into, teasing the value of sticking through the whole video.
4. **Main Content:** This is the meat of your video. Dive into detailed explanations, step-by-step tutorials, insights, or stories relevant to your solution and audience interests.
5. **Call to Action (CTA):** Always wrap up your video with a strong CTA. Encourage viewers to like, share, subscribe, or follow a link in the description. This is crucial for engagement and growth.

This template is like a skeleton. Your job is to add flesh to it with your unique content, style, and personality. Remember, the magic of faceless channels is that it's all about the content, not the creator. So, make sure your content is king.

Now, let's translate this template into a specific example. Say you're running a faceless channel about productivity hacks. Here's a script snippet to get your creative juices flowing:

"You've tried everything under the sun, but that monstrous to-do list just keeps growing. What if I told you there's a simple, yet insanely effective technique to slash your to-do list in half? Stick around as we dive deep into the '2-Minute Rule,' a life-changing productivity hack that you can start using today."

From there, you'd move into discussing the problem in depth, presenting the 2-Minute Rule, and guiding viewers on how to implement it. After providing vivid examples and perhaps some success stories, you'd round off with a CTA encouraging viewers to share their success stories with the 2-Minute Rule in the comments. Engaging, right?

Here's a quick tip: Don't underestimate the power of a well-crafted script. Writing down what you plan to say not only saves you tons of editing time but also helps you communicate more clearly and effectively.

Now, what about templates for different kinds of videos? Let's say you want to mix things up with a listicle, a comparison, or an explainer video. Each of these formats might require slight tweaks to the script structure but will fundamentally follow the same flow. A listicle, for example, would introduce the topic, list the items with details and engaging visuals (even in a faceless format), and end with a CTA. It's all about adapting while keeping your end goal in sight.

But wait, there's more. Templates aren't just about the script structure. They extend to your video thumbnails, titles, descriptions, and tags—essentially, your video's SEO. A good rule of thumb is to keep your titles clear and your thumbnails clickable without resorting to clickbait. Your descriptions should include keywords (naturally, please!) and a compelling reason for viewers to watch the video. Templates for these elements can save you a heap of time and boost your SEO efforts.

Before we wrap up, remember to sprinkle a bit of patience into the mix. Success on YouTube, especially with a faceless channel, doesn't happen overnight. Use these templates and scripts as your foundation, but always be ready to tweak and adjust based on what your analytics tell you. After all, the YouTube algorithm loves fresh, engaging content, but your audience's feedback is your true north.

So, there you have it. Armed with these templates and scripts, you're well on your way to creating engaging, value-packed content for your faceless YouTube channel. Keep your eyes on the prize—building a loyal viewership that fuels your passive income stream. Embrace the journey, learn from each video, and remember, consistency is key. Ready to make your mark? Let's get creating!

Checklists for Starting and Growing Your Channel

Embarking on the journey of launching a faceless YouTube channel is both thrilling and daunting. With a blend of creativity, strategy, and persistence, you're about to enter a world full of possibilities. Whether you're just jotting down video ideas or you're ready to hit the 'Publish' button, having a clear, structured plan is key to your channel's growth. That's what this checklist is all about – guiding you through the essentials, from the spark of an idea to a thriving channel.

First things first, have you defined your niche? Understanding the unique corner of YouTube your content will occupy is crucial. It shapes every decision you'll make moving forward. If you're still on the fence, it's time to dive deep into research, pinpointing areas you're passionate about, and evaluating their market demand. Your niche will be your north star, guiding your content creation.

Now, onto crafting your strategy. Setting clear, actionable goals will give you a roadmap to success. Think about what success looks like for your channel. Is it a certain number of subscribers? A level of monthly income? Whatever it is, write it down. Setting these milestones early helps in charting your progress.

Let's talk about the backbone of your channel – content. Developing a content calendar early on keeps you consistent, which is key on YouTube. Brainstorm content ideas, organize them into categories, and plan your publishing schedule. Remember, quality trumps quantity, but consistency is queen. Aim for a balance that you can realistically maintain.

As you're fleshing out your plans, don't overlook the technical setups, such as creating an engaging channel banner, picking a memorable name, and crafting a compelling channel description. These elements are often the first interaction people have with your channel, so make every word and image count.

Moving on to content creation, do you have your tools and processes in place? Whether it's scripting, recording voice-overs, or editing, each step requires its set of tools and software. Research the best options within your budget and ensure you're comfortable using them. Efficient workflows save you time and frustration, allowing you to focus on creating great content.

SEO - three letters that can make a big difference in your channel's visibility. Have you done your keyword research? Are your titles and descriptions optimized to catch both viewers' and YouTube's algorithm's eyes? Remember, SEO is an ongoing process. Always be on the lookout for trends and topics that resonate with your audience and incorporate relevant keywords naturally.

Uploading and publishing videos can't be done haphazardly. Consistency in your upload schedule helps build a loyal audience. Have you considered the best days and times to publish your videos? Utilizing YouTube's scheduled upload feature can help you stay on track without being glued to your computer.

Engagement is the currency of YouTube. Are you prepared to actively engage with your audience through comments, polls, and social media? Building a community around your channel not only boosts your channel's visibility but also fosters a loyal viewer base.

Partnerships and collaborations can propel your channel forward. Start identifying other creators or brands that align with your content for potential collaborations. Remember, collaborations are a two-way street; think about what you can offer them in return.

Monetization is often a primary goal for creators. Have you explored all the avenues for making money on YouTube? Beyond AdSense, consider affiliate marketing, sponsorships, or even launching your own merchandise. Diversifying your income sources can provide financial stability for your channel.

Staying ahead of the curve is what keeps your channel relevant. Are you keeping an eye on new YouTube features and trends that you can incorporate into your own strategy? Being adaptable and willing to experiment can set you apart from competitors.

Lastly, remember the power of analytics. YouTube provides a wealth of data about your videos and audience. Make it a routine to review your performance metrics, learn what works, and adjust your strategies accordingly. Data-driven decisions can significantly impact your channel's growth.

Creating and growing a faceless YouTube channel is an evolution, not a one-time setup. It's about iterating, refining, and most importantly, learning as you go. Embrace the process, celebrate your milestones (no matter how small), and stay committed to your vision.

Don't let the weight of perfectionism hold you back. The best time to start is now, and the best way to learn is by doing. Each video you create, each strategy you employ, and each milestone you reach brings you one step closer to mastering the art of running a successful faceless YouTube channel.

Remember, success on YouTube is a unique journey for every creator. Yours will be filled with its own set of challenges and triumphs. Keep pushing forward, stay true to your vision, and let your passion shine through your content. The road to building a thriving, passive income-generating channel is in front of you. Are you ready to take the first step?

Glossary of YouTube and Digital Marketing Terms

As you navigate the world of faceless YouTube channels and explore the vast ocean of digital marketing, you're going to come across a whirlwind of terms that might have you scratching your head. Fret not! Below you'll find a rundown of essential terms that'll not only make you sound like you've been in the game for years but also arm you with the knowledge to turn your passive income dreams into a reality.

Affiliate Marketing

It's when you promote someone else's products or services, and in return, you get a commission for every sale made through your unique referral link. Think of it as being a middleman, but without the tedious paperwork.

Algorithm

The brain behind YouTube's operation. It's a complex set of rules that determines which videos get promoted on the platform and to whom they get shown. Cracking the code on this can get your content in front of the right eyes.

Click-Through Rate (CTR)

This metric tells you the percentage of people who see your video's thumbnail and then actually click on it. High CTR? You're on the right track. Low CTR? Time to rethink your thumbnail or title strategy.

Content Calendar

It's your battle plan. A schedule that outlines what content you're going to publish and when. It helps keep you organized and ensures that you're consistently delivering the goods to your audience.

Engagement Rate

This is all about interaction. Likes, comments, shares, and even the length of time viewers watch your videos contribute to this metric. It's a solid indicator of how well your content resonates with your audience.

Keywords

These are the golden nuggets of SEO (Search Engine Optimization). Keywords are words or phrases that people use to search for content on YouTube. Including these in your video titles, descriptions, and tags can help your videos get discovered.

Monetization

The moment your channel starts making money. Through ads, sponsorships, or even selling your own merchandise, monetization is the turning point where your channel goes from hobby to income generator.

Niche

Your sweet spot. It's the specific topic or area you focus your channel on. Finding the right niche can help you attract a dedicated audience and build authority in that space.

SEO (Search Engine Optimization)

The art and science of making your content discoverable. By optimizing your videos for keywords, improving engagement rates, and creating quality content, you increase your chances of appearing in search results and recommended video feeds.

Thumbnail

The first impression of your video. This small but mighty image can make or break your video's success. A compelling thumbnail grabs attention and encourages viewers to click through to your content.

Grasping these terms is just the beginning. As you dive deeper into your journey, you'll come to see that these aren't just buzzwords; they're your tools for building a successful faceless YouTube channel that generates passive income. Keep experimenting, learning, and, above all, creating. The digital world is vast, and the possibilities are endless.

Resources for Further Assistance

Embarking on your journey into the world of faceless YouTube channels and digital marketing can feel like navigating through uncharted waters. That's precisely why having a compass in the form of resources and assistance can turn what seems like a daunting venture into a thrilling adventure. There's an ocean of information out there, but let's dive into the most impactful resources that can guide you toward success.

Firstly, there are countless YouTube channels dedicated to educating creators about the nuances of YouTube and digital marketing. These channels provide everything from basic tutorials to deep dives into strategy and analytics. Subscribing to them is like having a mentor guide you every step of the way. The trick is to filter through and find those that resonate with your learning style and content creation philosophy.

Online forums and communities are another goldmine for advice and support. Platforms like Reddit have dedicated subreddits for YouTube creators and digital marketing, where you can ask questions, share experiences, and connect with like-minded individuals. Engaging in these communities not only helps you gain insights but also builds a support network that can be invaluable as you grow.

Blogs and websites dedicated to the art and science of YouTube creation and digital marketing are a resource you can't afford to overlook. These sites often post up-to-date information on algorithm changes, strategies for audience engagement, and much more. Bookmarking your favorites for easy reference can keep you informed and inspired.

Books, both digital and physical, written by experienced creators and marketers, can provide comprehensive knowledge and insights that you might not find elsewhere. They compile the wisdom of years into a format that's detailed yet accessible. Keep an eye out for titles that come highly recommended by others in the field.

Podcasts related to YouTube strategy and digital marketing are perfect for creators on the go. Listening to these can turn your commute or downtime into a productive learning session. The conversational tone often used in podcasts makes complex topics easier to digest and understand.

Don't underestimate the power of online courses and workshops. These can range from free introductory sessions to comprehensive paid programs offering certificates. Designed by experts, they're structured to take you from the basics all the way to advanced techniques in a coherent and systematic way.

Utilizing the analytics tools offered by YouTube itself can also serve as a great resource. Learning to interpret the data provided by YouTube Analytics can give you insights into what works and what doesn't, allowing you to refine your strategy over time.

For those who thrive on direct interaction, attending digital marketing conferences and creator meetups can be enormously beneficial. These events not only offer learning opportunities but also provide networking avenues that could lead to collaborations and partnerships.

Software and tools specific to video creation, SEO optimization, and channel management can also serve as resources. Many of these tools have their own tutorials, blogs, and support communities, which can be an additional layer of assistance.

Social media platforms themselves can be untapped resources. Following thought leaders and joining groups focused on YouTube growth and digital marketing can provide daily nuggets of wisdom and innovative ideas to try on your channel.

Email newsletters from digital marketing experts and platforms can be a concise way to receive updates and tips right in your inbox. Subscribing to a select few ensures you're always in the loop on the latest trends and best practices.

Webinars and live streams by seasoned creators and marketers offer real-time learning opportunities. These sessions often include Q&A segments where you can get direct responses to your queries.

Mentorship programs, whereby experienced creators take you under their wing, can accelerate your learning curve. While finding a mentor can be challenging, the personalised guidance and feedback make it worth the effort.

Lastly, experimenting and learning from your own experiences can be the most powerful resource. Every successful creator has a trail of trials, errors, and learning moments. Embrace the journey, keep iterating, and use each video as a stepping stone towards mastery.

Remember, the world of YouTube and digital marketing is always evolving. Staying curious, open to learning, and willing to adapt are your best strategies for success. Use these resources as your toolkit, and don't hesitate to forge your own path. After all, the next breakthrough strategy could very well come from you.

www.ingramcontent.com/pod-product-compliance
Lightning Source LLC
Chambersburg PA
CBHW050215230526
45470CB00001B/403